D1117958

Fantasy
and
Imagination
in the
Mexican
Narrative

Fantasy and Imagination in the Mexican Narrative

BY
ROSS LARSON

Published by
Center for Latin American Studies
Arizona State University
Tempe

Library of Congress Cataloging in Publication Data

Larson, Ross.
  Fantasy and imagination in the Mexican narrative.

  Bibliography: p.
  1. Mexican fiction — History and criticism.
  2. Supernatural in literature. I. Title.
  PQ7207.S8L3   863'.009   77-3019
  ISBN 0-87918-013-5
  ISBN 0-87918-032-3 pbk.

Copyright © 1977 — Arizona Board of Regents
Arizona State University
Center for Latin American Studies
Tempe, Arizona 85281

All rights reserved. No part of this publication may be
reproduced or transmitted in any form or by any
means, electronic or mechanical, including photo-
copy, recording, or any information storage or re-
trieval system, without permission in writing from
the publisher.

Published in the United States of America.

Typeset by Techno Logue Corporation

Printed by Publishers Press, Inc.

Bookbinding by Roswell Bookbinding

Bureau of Publications • 677

ROBERT MANNING
STROZIER LIBRARY

MAY 7 1991

Tallahassee, Florida

For Carolyn

Contents

Preface

The purpose of the present study is to examine the substantial body of literature of fantasy and imagination produced in Mexico and thus to contribute to a better understanding of the nature of Mexican prose fiction. Since no other systematic treatment of the subject has yet appeared, this investigation serves a definite need. The findings, it will be seen, are in opposition to the prevailing idea that Mexican narrative works not characterized by objective realism and explicit social purpose are both extremely rare and insignificant.[1]

The essential concepts underlying the organization of the study —namely, fantasy and imagination—should immediately be clarified. While it is true that all fiction is imaginary by definition, we are here concerned particularly with that class of fiction which breaks with the common view of experienced reality. The physical universe may be scarcely recognizable in works of fantasy and imagination, for the constituent elements have arbitrarily been recombined for a special effect. Such a uniquely distorted representation may be an author's means of communicating a deeply personal, even a visionary experience of reality (imagination); alternatively, the novelty may be an end in itself, a whimsical invention designed only to please or excite the reader (fantasy), and not to enlighten him. The boundary between fantasy and imagination often is not so readily discernible; yet, an effort has been made to adhere rigorously to the distinction as outlined in *Webster's New World Dictionary*:

> *Imagination* is often regarded as the more seriously and deeply creative faculty, which perceives the basic resemblances between things, as distinguished from *Fancy*, the lighter and more decorative faculty, which perceives superficial resemblances.[2]

And again, more fully elaborated, in *Webster's New Collegiate Dictionary:*

> *Imagination, fancy, fantasy* mean the power to form mental images of things not before one, or the exercise of that power in literature and art. *Imagination*, the general and, usually, underogatory term, may apply to the mental representation of that which is remembered (reproductive imagination) or of that which has never been (especially in its entirety) presented to the senses (often called creative imagination): in this latter sense, *fancy* is now, sometimes, its equivalent, but is more often distinguished, *imagination* being the power to represent the real more fully and truly than it appears to the senses and in its ideal or universal character, and *fancy* to the power of inventing the novel and unreal by recombining the elements of reality; *fantasy* applies to the power of unrestrained (often extravagant or delusive) fancy, especially as exhibited in art.[3]

The scope of this investigation extends to all periods of Mexican literary history, but certain deliberate omissions and inclusions will need to be explained. The most obvious omission, that of children's literature, is justified by the fact that this is perhaps the only aspect of our subject which has already been well investigated, notably by Blanca Lydia Trejo.[4] Pre-Columbian myths and legends that have been gathered and translated into Spanish lie beyond the range of this study, as do the tales brought from Spain, except for those that have suffered modification from contact with the New World. The inclusion of a few authors not actually born in Mexico is unlikely to be disputed. Bernardo de Balbuena, José de la Colina, Arturo Souto Alabarce, and Elena Poniatowska all were brought to Mexico when they were children, and thus their writings can be classified only as Mexican. The work of Joaquín Bolaños is studied because, although he may have come to Mexico as an adult, no literary background in Spain has ever been attributed to him. And Alfredo Cardona Peña, for many years an important figure in the literature of Mexico, is included despite the claim asserted by his native Costa Rica. Nevertheless, other non-Mexicans who are authors of literary fantasies and residents of Mexico are excluded; they remain outside the current of Mexican literature.

The material for the study was gradually accumulated during two-and-a-half years spent in Mexico. These works of fantasy and imagination were discovered in second-hand bookshops, private libraries, the Biblioteca Nacional, the Hemeroteca Nacional, the Colegio de México, and the library of the Facultad de Filosofía y Letras in the Universidad Nacional Autónoma de México. The study is organized according to a thematic grouping of the 743 works as follows: Part I, dealing with Fantasy, is subdivided into four chapters: Fear and the Supernatural, Legend and Christian Myths, Literary Divertissements, and Utopian and Science Fiction; Part II, on literature of Imagination, comprises three chapters: The Unconscious, Expressionism, and Magical Realism. It is worth emphasizing that the present work has a broad focus and that its basic aim has been the *exposition* and *description* of a particular mode of literature in Mexico. The approach is mainly extensive rather than intensive, and yet some critical analysis and appraisal is made, particularly of the cardinal authors of the two sections—Francisco Tario as the outstanding proponent of Fantasy, with Juan José Arreola and Carlos Fuentes representing literature of Imagination.

This first comprehensive survey of fantasy and imagination in the Mexican narrative makes no claim to end the need for further investigation, but simply charts an area long neglected by literary criticism. The detailed bibliography which is provided will assist future investigators who might undertake to examine more closely the many works that have been undeservedly ignored.

Acknowledgments

The author wishes to acknowledge his indebtedness to the many people both in Mexico and Canada who contributed in many ways to the progress of this study. Sincere appreciation is due to Kurt L. Levy for his generous encouragement and advice, and to Robert J. Glickman and Keith Ellis for their thorough reading of the preliminary draft and for their helpful suggestions for its improvement. The gratitude of the author is likewise expressed to Pedro Frank De Andrea, María Elvira Bermúdez and Emmanuel Carballo for valuable cooperation and assistance given during the period of research in Mexico City. Special acknowledgment is made to the Canada Council and the Ontario Provincial Government for their financial support.

Part 1
Fantasy

---------- CHAPTER 1 ----------

Fear and the Supernatural

Fear is man's most primitive emotion. Whatever lies beyond his ability to comprehend or to influence has usually inspired him with dread. Early man learned to cope with his environment by hypothesizing in each element and force of nature a personal spirit with which he could bargain in human terms. Even more sophisticated religious systems, while supposing the universe to be the instrument of a single supreme intelligence, retain a propitiatory relation with the deity in their divinely-inspired codes of moral conduct. Thus convinced of the order in all things and assured that members of society will act in the manner prescribed, one can feel secure and even complacent. Consequently, any experience of the supernatural—whether direct or indirect—challenges this tidy conception of reality. It produces a feeling of uneasiness often accompanied by a physical shudder, which Freud has sought to explain in his paper on "The Uncanny":

> Nowadays we have surmounted these [animistic]...modes of thought; but we do not feel quite sure of our new beliefs, and the old ones still exist within us ready to seize upon any confirmation. As soon as something *actually* happens in our lives which seems to confirm the old, discarded beliefs we get a feeling of the uncanny; and it is as though we were making a judgment something like this: "So, after all it is true that one can kill a person by the mere wish!" or, "So the dead do live on and appear on the scene of their former activities!" and so on.[1]

Hence the audience most appreciative of eerie tales is comprised of those who are basically undecided about the authenticity of super-normal phenomena. Readers who have definitely surmounted superstitious beliefs, by contrast, are impatient with accounts of the supernatural and will tend to view such literature as the product of a delusion or as simply preposterous. At the opposite extreme is a third group of readers, namely, those who believe implicitly that the laws of nature may be suspended at any time by some superior agency. The credulous, then, and the frankly skeptical alike fail to respond emotionally to the supernatural elements that are central to these tales.

Most authors who deal in the supernatural seek only to evoke the shudder, the sense of the uncanny—a goal that is quite easily achieved. One can illustrate how a single motif can be made to serve effectively again and again in varied circumstances. For example, the animistic association between an object and its owner is observed in a number of stories. In "Los dos cedros" (1922) by Manuel Romero de Terreros, two trees are planted in front of their house by a newly-wed couple. The husband's death years later coincides with that of one of the cedars. The widow goes to live in Europe after selling the house to the narrator, who has agreed to take special care of the remaining cedar. Yet despite his efforts the tree withers and dies. While the narrator is considering whether to notify the woman, he happens to see notice of her death in a Paris newspaper. Carlos Toro repeats the motif in "El árbol de los caracoles" (1947), a sentimental tale about a sickly young girl who dies when her favorite tree is uprooted. A child in Salvador Calvillo Madrigal's trivial story "Tabú" (1952) breaks a cuckoo clock he had been forbidden to touch. At that instant his grandfather in the next room cries out and falls dead.

Francisco Rojas González achieves notable artistic success when, in "Mateo el Evangelista" (1946), he uses the device to express the inner tragedy of a sensitive and humble escribano público. Every day Mateo sits at a sidewalk table typing letters for the poor and uneducated. The emotions of all the people pass through him and he involves himself deeply and sympathetically with each of their problems. He writes their love letters, their family letters, their legal letters. One day a stranger comes to his table and asks him to type the brief tragic message "No se culpe a nadie mi muerte." On the following day Mateo is found dead and his typewriter can not be made to function.

The uncanny sensation, as we have seen, can be provoked more or less automatically, since it relies primarily on the beliefs held by the reader. It is the author's art that determines the success or failure of any story, of course, but, as in the traditional ballad, fiction involving the supernatural is often left undeveloped beyond the skeletal stage of the anecdote. Stories of suggestion and the ineffable qualities of existence, however, make more demands on the writer and generally are more satisfying to the critical reader. Romero de Terreros establishes a pervasive, eerie atmosphere surrounding a mysterious and ominous box in "El cofre" (1922). The box contains only a piece of paper, but we never learn what is written on the paper, for the old man who reads it dies instantly and it drops into the fire. The revelation of one of life's mysteries is thwarted again by death in another of his stories: "Similia similibus" (1922).

Public interest in spiritualism is most prevalent during periods of social upheaval and especially in war-time, when large numbers of bereaved seek consolation and reassurance about the welfare of departed souls. Religion offers limited comfort, for it speaks only of the probability of spiritual survival, whereas spiritualism claims unreservedly to provide actual communication with the spirit world. In times of turmoil and reassessment of values, it is natural to ask whether there might not be something beyond material existence. Unpleasant circumstances are made tolerable by a belief in ultimate salvation. The Romantic idealists associated with the turbulent period of the Reform in Mexico—covering roughly the second third of the nineteenth century—exalted the phenomenon of love and the intuitive power of the imagination far above the processes of reason. Thus, the subject of spiritualism naturally fascinated Romantic authors like Justo Sierra and, later, the Modernists as well, for Modernism began essentially as a repudiation of the mechanistic theory of life that was current during a time of capitalistic expansion and material prosperity for the privileged minority under the dictatorship of Porfirio Díaz. Affirmation of a hidden realm of the spirit, accessible only to the artist and poet, is fundamental in Rubén Darío's first important work, *Azul* (1888), as Juan Valera observed:

> Que en ese infinito tenebroso e incognoscible perciba la imaginación, así como en el éter, nebulosas o semilleros de astros, fragmentos y escombros de religiones muertas, con los cuales procura formar algo como ensayo de nuevas creencias y de renovadas mitologías.[2]

The oriental concept of successive rebirths in a process of self-perfection exactly suited the temperament of both the Romantics and the Modernists: they too were in search of an Absolute, an Ideal. Justo Sierra wrote the sentimental fantasy "Incógnita" (1868) to dramatize the belief that for everyone there exists a twin soul which he is destined to meet in one of his lives. Amado Nervo was less confident of the possibility of ideal love on earth. Rafael, the sensitive, rather neurotic protagonist of *El donador de almas* (1899) is given a soul, Alda, thus providing him with the chance for a perfect intellectual relationship. At first Alda and Rafael's own soul are happy sharing Rafael's head. But inevitably Rafael's physical desires lead to internal conflict. The setting of Nervo's typically Modernist novel shifts from Russia to France, then to Italy, Egypt and the Holy Land, yet the struggle is entirely psychological and amounts to a confrontation between worldly and spiritual love. Upon releasing Alda, the unfortunate hero finds his love for her renewed. He feels her presence in the wind and longs to join her through death. From a suitable distance the Ideal can be sustained and serve as a pretext for pathetic melancholy.

The Pythagorean and oriental theme of metempsychosis was first employed in Mexico by José María Roa Bárcena in "El rey y el bufón" (1882), a morality tale where an exchange of souls for one year between a king and his jester seriously alters the souls themselves: the mighty ruler's soul turns pious and meek in its new circumstances; that of the affable fool becomes petulant and anarchistic. After Modernism, the transmigration of souls and their reincarnation occurs only in grim and appalling tales, at least, until Francisco Tario [Francisco Peláez] takes up the theme and deflates its solemnity.

An atmosphere of menace surrounds the protagonist of "Un inefable rumor" (1968), who is terrorized by an unidentifiable sound. Tario gradually increases the tension, then suddenly destroys it in an absurd anticlimax. The sound is only a cricket—actually the protagonist himself in his new existence. In another burlesque, "Fuera de programa" (1968), Tario tells the love story of a girl and a horse and of her providential reincarnation as a sleek white mare. The transmigration-of-souls motif is also present in "Ciclopropano" (1952) to ridicule materialism and provides the final twist to the involved plot of "Aureola o alvéolo" (1950), the strange account of the search by Norway's foremost ghost-hunter for the ghost of an Irishman he thinks he had murdered, but who, he learns, had actually murdered him. "Aureola o alvéolo" seems to parody the metaphysical detective literature of Jorge Luis Borges, but in itself it is an amusing and intriguing ghost story.

Prominent among those who helped to prepare the way for the Mexican Revolution and the defeat of Porfirio Díaz was a young lawyer and newspaper editor named José Vasconcelos. In 1920 Vasconcelos was appointed Secretary of Public Education under President Obregón, a post which he held until 1929, when he abandoned politics for philosophy and literature. A basic assumption of his philosophical system is that reality as a whole is composed of energy and that its nature can best be comprehended through the emotional experience of that special form of cosmic energy we call beauty. The idea that music in particular enables man to integrate himself with the mysteries[3] is illustrated in "La sonata mágica" (1933), where a composer is demonstrating to some friends how successfully he has captured all the sounds of creation when suddenly a bolt of lightning crashes through the roof, strikes the piano, and consumes the sheet of music. A vestige of such emotional aestheticism is found in Sergio Larrea Rionoso's "Los vientos sonoros" (1968). This recent story tells of a herdsman who devises a marvelous flute that is in fact a replica of the world in miniature. When the flute is played, all of nature surrenders its energy, which is transformed into acoustic vibrations that leave the region totally barren and dead.

The idea of a spiritual realm co-existing with our own but beyond our normal powers of perception is widely accepted, as it accounts for apparently inexplicable supernatural phenomena. This so-called "fourth dimension" takes its name from the geometry of hyperspace, where mathematicians assume the existence of additional dimensions in order to explain equations containing more than three unknowns. Fanciful descriptions of such a hypothetical region inevitably reflect their authors' interests and desires. José Vasconcelos deals with it in "La casa imantada" (1933), which concerns a young man whose girl is snatched from him and carried off by some invisible power. While searching for her, he too is caught by the strange force and pulled into a deserted house. Then he finds himself in an enchanted garden where miraculously he can comprehend the essence of all things:

> Una dulce paz colmaba de bienestar sus sentidos. Se acercó a las cosas pretendiendo tocarlas y sintió que las penetraba, pero sin deshacerlas ni deshacerse en ellas; estaba como en el interior de todo, y, sin embargo, cada objeto conservaba su perfil y su propia substancia. . . . Todo lo entendía y sentía como si su propio ser animase y desenvolviese el conjunto. El paisaje entero, las plantas y el ambiente le parecían suyos de una manera que jamás había sospechado. . . . De pronto, en medio de su profunda voluptuosidad, tuvo este pensamiento: ¡Oh, si ella se encontrase en el jardín! Cómo la penetraría en toda su substancia, cómo lograría entonces lo que nunca han podido conseguir de una manera absoluta sin destruirse.[4]

Many writers are less optimistic about the nature of the fourth dimension, and present it as an eerie and sinister realm to be avoided. A female image in a stream bewitches and lures a young man to his death in a story by Felipe Montilla Duarte, "Alma de agua" (1955)— essentially the same legend that Bécquer heard in Spain and recorded in 1871 as "Los ojos verdes." But Montilla Duarte sets it in Yucatán and even transcribes the regional dialect ("No te acerquej ar río que

suj aguaj embrujan . . . ahí va uno máj que se ha ío pa se Alma er Agua
. . .").[5] The reflection cast by water or a mirror is itself uncanny.

Numerous folk motifs are inspired by the supposed relation between a person and his image[6]—ego and alter ego, matter and spirit—
and these in turn provide the theme for fantasy stories such as Amado
Nervo's "El del espejo" (1909), in which a man dies shot in the head
after he fires at his reflection. Occasionally, the spiritual world can be
glimpsed in a mirror (Amparo Dávila, "El espejo," 1956) and some
people—like Alice—can physically penetrate the mirror (Ana de
Gómez Mayorga, "El espejo," 1946), at the risk, however, of being
trapped in the other dimension if the mirror is shattered behind them
(Francisco Tario in "Asesinato en do sostenido mayor," 1968, and in
"T.S.H.," 1952, achieves a characteristic, grotesque result by present-
ing this nightmarish theme with irresistible humor). Fictional characters find, to their horror, that by simply passing through a doorway
(Ana de Gómez Mayorga, "La puerta," 1946; Cristina Ruiz "La puerta
secreta," 1968) or riding on a train (Ana de Gómez Mayorga, "El
viaje," 1946) they have slipped into a strange unknown world where
they are trapped. In most cases, they are never heard from again. As
usual, Tario provides a notable exception. "La polka de los Curitas"
(1952) is the hilarious account of a strange epidemic that spreads
among nearly the entire population of a town. The only symptom or
warning seems to be the sound of the town band (themselves the first
victims) playing a certain polka. Within a few minutes of hearing the
music, each victim vanishes:

> Modistas, jornaleros, escribientes, abogados, concejales, sirvientas . . .
> unos tras otros caían enfermos y desaparecían. Y cayó al fin el doctor. Y
> el párroco. Y el alcalde se esfumó una noche de su casa, con un
> bocadillo de jamón en la mano. Se clausuraron los espectáculos y las
> carnicerías, se prohibieron cierta clase de pescados, las reuniones
> públicas fueron suspendidas y se exigió que se cocieran las frutas.
> También, bajo pena de muerte, se prohibió escupir en las calles y en la
> pastelería. Sobre los muros de los principales edificios aparecieron
> pasquines significativos: *Cuídese usted de la polka. La polka no es lo
> que todos suponen, sino una enfermedad misteriosa y muy grave.* El
> Ayuntamiento, al cabo, resolvió substituir aquellos pegostes: *La polka
> no causa la muerte. La horrible gravitación os espera.* Prevengámonos
> de las zanahorias.[7]

After a few months, letters begin to arrive from the victims, who are
well and having a wonderful time—in Yaksu, Tibet! Before long the
remaining few townspeople are trying to contract the polka so they
too can go. The eerie fourth dimension is reduced by Francisco Tario
to a fantastic travel service.

H. G. Wells with his "scientific fantasy," *The Time Machine* (1895), is chiefly responsible for an alternative view, where the fourth dimension is conceived of as a dimension of time rather than as a spatial entity. Works that involve the use of machines for travel in the time dimension or space-time continuum will not be presented here, but will be discussed in a later chapter devoted to science fiction. The limitations of time can be transcended in fantasy, however, without any need for elaborate machines. There are Mexican folk traditions of phantom cities from the past that, like mirages, may appear to the solitary wayfarer. Manuel Romero de Terreros's "El camino de los carboneros" (1922) tells of a footpath that leads back into the seventeenth century. The future is revealed by means of special optical surgery in *El sexto sentido* (1918) by Amado Nervo; and Diego Cañedo allows his characters to view the past through magic spectacles in *Isolda o el misterio de las gafas verdes* (1952).

Yet even without the benefit of magical devices or operations, such visions are purportedly experienced. María Elvira Bermúdez imagines herself traveling in Europe apparently along the same route followed by a certain Dutchman three centuries earlier. Again and again she receives his sensations, thoughts and memories. The title of the story, "Agujeros en la nada" (1965), is taken from a discussion by the physicist George Gamow of Paul Dirac's theory that led to the discovery of particles in space known as positrons.[8] Bermúdez suggests that Dirac's "holes in empty space" are not void but are filled with memory, an idea that ultimately is related to the spiritualist theory that objects absorb and retain vibrations from their surroundings and hence are capable of recreating scenes from the past.

Similarly, the individual himself is thought to be a source of emanating vibrations that reverberate indefinitely and that can be received at any time by a psychically sensitive percipient. During the Second World War, Rafael Solana suggested a practical application of this psychical phenomenon. "El arma secreta" (1944) concerns a weapon which might have enabled Hitler to rule the world. A Nazi psychologist named Keller has measured the actual force that can be exerted by the human mind:

> Un hombre, deseando fuertemente una cosa, con una concentración de su voluntad, produce una fuerza psíquica que he denominado "kellerina"; una kellerina puede hacer moverse ligeramente una cortina de gasa; diez kellerinas son capaces de desviar a una mosca en su camino; cien kellerinas atraen una carta perdida a su destino, mil kellerinas consiguen que el trapecista que iba a caer alcance en el aire el trapecio y se salve, y, para abreviar, diez millones de kellerinas pueden matar a un hombre a distancia.[9]

If the German people are ordered to concentrate their thoughts on specific Allied leaders at designated times, victory will be assured. But Hitler is too shrewd to risk his own life by letting the people have this secret weapon.

Death itself is perhaps the ultimate mystery of human existence, the final question that has always fascinated mankind. In Mexican culture there seems to be little of the fear and anguish that Western society has come to associate with the theme. Instead, the Mexican maintains a notoriously casual attitude towards death, an attitude which, according to Octavio Paz, is a consequence of his traditional lack of self esteem:

> El desprecio a la muerte no está reñido con el culto que le profesamos. Ella está presente en nuestras fiestas, en nuestros juegos, en nuestros amores y en nuestros pensamientos. Morir y matar son ideas que pocas veces nos abandonan. La muerte nos seduce. La fascinación que ejerce sobre nosotros quizá brote de nuestro hermetismo y de la furia con que lo rompemos. . . . En un mundo cerrado y sin salida, en donde todo es muerte, lo único valioso es la muerte. Pero afirmamos algo negativo. Calaveras de azúcar o de papel de China, esqueletos coloridos de fuegos de artificio, nuestras representaciones populares son siempre burla de la vida, afirmación de la nadería e insignificancia de la humana existencia. Adornamos nuestras casas con cráneos, comemos el día de los Difuntos panes que fingen huesos y nos divierten canciones y chascarrillos en los que ríe la muerte pelona, pero toda esa fanfarrona familiaridad no nos dispensa de la pregunta que todos nos hacemos: ¿qué es la muerte? No hemos inventado una nueva respuesta. Y cada vez que nos la preguntamos, nos encogemos de hombros: ¿qué me importa la muerte, si no me importa la vida?[10]

Testimony regarding the nature of death has been borne by several living corpses in Mexican literature, but their statements tend to be frivolous or tendentious. Julio Torri's brief sketch in rhythmic prose "La vida del campo" (1917) is a waggish satire of bucolic verse after the example of Manuel Acuña's poem of the same title. While being carted along the road from town to the cemetery (*camposanto*), a corpse confides to a drunken mourner that it is quite looking forward to its new home. It will make new friends and listen to the birds. "La vida del campo," it says, "tiene también sus atractivos."[11] José Vasconcelos, slightly more serious, resurrects a dead soldier in "El fusilado" (1919) in order to portray death as a liberation from life's troubles and to ridicule the pretentions of spiritualism. Truth is not found in what seems to be supernatural, says Vasconcelos, but rather "en la inspiración del genio y en el secreto de los sueños."[12] He alludes to the essence of truth in his final assertion: "descubrirán . . .

que . . . no rigen las leyes corrientes, sino la ley estética, la ley de la más elevada fantasía."[13]

The theme of death finds a sober fictional treatment in a work by María Elvira Bermúdez, *Soliloquio de un muerto* (1951), the title of which indicates both the form of narration and the ancient device of examining life from the point of view of death. A corpse, conscious enough to frame thoughts, expresses delight in the unlimited horizon of the grave and its quiet solitude. It disdains the living for their misleading reliance upon words to formulate philosophical concepts. The religious are particularly derided on account of their greedy desire for eternal life, along with those who believe death to be a passing into nothingness: obviously they are mistaken. But gradually the story's controlled reasoning becomes unsteady and the syntax begins to disintegrate. Then at last there is only silence. The corpse, we suppose, has entered the final stage in the process of dying. The effort to understand death is at root an oblique expression of the will to understand life. On such a mission Bermúdez follows the transit of a woman's soul into death in "La oscuridad primordial" (1966). All the gods of ancient Greek, Roman, and Mexican mythology are waiting to judge her. Tezcatlipoca, the Aztec god of fate, leads her back through the decisive moments of her life until her one crucial error is discovered. This woman's tragic destiny was to ignore the only offer of love she would receive and to waste her life begging love of those who had none to give.

Often the dead narrator merely provides a convenient vantage point from which to view reality. José Rubén Romero uses the device to satirize his mourners in *Anticipación a la muerte* (1939). Unfortunately, the author's humor is overextended and the novel fails. Another instance of such reliance upon a device to compensate for a superficial treatment is "Mi velorio," a trivial piece by Juan Vicente Melo in which a dead youth tries to revive, but is held firmly in the coffin by his family. The story no doubt had symbolic importance for its author, whose parents, we know, compelled him to follow the family tradition and study medicine; they always opposed his desire to become a professional writer. He received his medical degree in 1956, the year this story was published. Two years later he finally broke with medicine and with his family.[14]

All the motifs and many of the plots for stories of the supernatural are furnished by popular tradition. Witchcraft tales like "Un viaje al más allá" (1953) and "La hechicera" (1964) by Raquel Banda Farfán may seem closer to folklore than to fiction. Indeed her stories' charm rests precisely on the authentic popular flavor with which they are infused. For the scientific study of folk tales, determination of the extent of any personal invention is vitally important. But literary value depends upon the way material is employed, not upon its source. The title-character of "María 'La voz' " (1939) is a girl possessed. With the aid of her guardian spirit, she does business as the village diviner until enemies succeed in killing her. Subsequently, it is rumored that the "voice" has entered the body of a girl in another village. Juan de la Cabada demonstrates in this short story how a poet can transform a commonplace rural tale into a work of extraordinary beauty and psychological insight.[15]

When María Elvira Bermúdez visited the macabre gallery of mummies displayed in the crypt beneath Guanajuato's cemetery, she was moved to write a much less lyrical story of superstition. In "Así es morir" (1953), she relates the mental anguish experienced by a man who lets himself be locked in the crypt overnight to win a bet. In the morning his friends discover that he has vanished and in his place there is a new mummy. The use of first person narration effectively forces the reader to share in the protagonists's mounting terror. This popular belief that mockery of the dead will bring horrible retribution is reiterated by José Guadalupe Herrera Carrillo in "Míster Parkington aprende a reír" (1962). Míster Parkington, a wealthy American businessman, visits the same underground burial vault in Guanajuato and, as a joke, he places his pipe in the mouth of a mummy who was reputed to have been a witch. Later, while smoking his pipe, he is stricken with an unaccountable illness: his face becomes paralyzed and his lips begin to decay. With his bleeding gums and half-eaten face he appears to be making a grotesque laugh. It is not his laugh, however, but that of someone inside him laughing at him.

Even when tales of terror lack any supernatural element, they are closely related to the marvelous. The supernatural and the unnatural alike are associated with a religious view of life. The Christian heresy of witchcraft and the horrible mental and physical torture of some innocents are both actions so evil as to challenge the divine order in nature. Both evoke the same secret, uncanny thrills in the reader whose measured daily routine allows him but little scope for expressing his erotic and aggressive impulses. The artist does not have to repress his anxieties; he can give them a shape, objectify them in a work of art and possibly escape the fate of neurosis. The reader or viewer who participates in the artist's fantasy also achieves a degree of catharsis.

Mexico's master of terror was Alejandro Cuevas, who, early in this century, appalled and delighted readers of the illustrated Sunday supplement to *El Diario* with his series of "Cuentos macabros," which combine elements of violence, evil, and eroticism. The correlation that exists between these ingredients is emphasized by Georges Bataille throughout his study *L'Érotique*. For example,

> le marquis de Sade définit dans le meurtre un sommet de l'excitation érotique. . . . Il y a dans le passage de l'attitude normale au désir une fascination fondamentale de la mort. Ce qui est en jeu dans l'érotisme est toujours une dissolution des formes constituées.[16]

The short story "Cordelia" (1911) with its stock heroine—young, beautiful, and virgin—epitomizes the work of Cuevas. The girl's real name is Consuelo, but for the narrator she is Cordelia because of her constant devotion to her father—a demented old man who sings unceasingly a morbid song about a carpenter and a coffin. On the eve of Good Friday, Cordelia decides to have an altar built in the house as is the Mexican custom. The narrator furnishes the building materials, including two very long spikes. The following morning he is awakened by screams from Cordelia's house. There he finds the old man sitting on Cordelia's body, singing his song and gaily driving one of the spikes through Cordelia's skull. The reader is at once titillated and horrified by such a mockery of the crucifixion, by the rapacious destruction of life and beauty and by the implication of incest.

Cuevas in another grisly story, "El fin de Mariana" (1908), tells of a virtuous woman who has become subject to attacks of loss of memory, paralysis, and mutism. Lying on her bed one day in a state of paralysis, she sees three rats climb onto her. They begin to chew her clothes and then her flesh. She can only watch in terror as they devour her alive. Days later her skeleton is discovered. In "Carboncillo" (1908), Cuevas tells of an Indian lad who is contracted to leave his village and go to Mérida on a brief job. While he is there, news comes from home that his young wife has died and been buried. Years later, unable to maintain the rental of the cemetery plot, he is forced to exhume his wife's body. When he opens the coffin, he discovers her in a horrible twisted position and with an expression of terror on her face. Her bridal veil is stained with the blood that dripped from her hands as she clawed at the lid and at her cheeks.

Horror fiction offers an aesthetic enjoyment that accounts for the genre's wide popularity. Our self-confidence increases and we are secretly pleased to witness any disaster—an automobile accident, a ship in distress, or a house afire—not because someone else is suffering, but because we ourselves are safe.[17] Even the sound of rain on the roof has this pleasing effect on us, but when the action seems morbid or depraved our ideas of common morality rush forward and may impair our aesthetic response. Baudelaire's observation that "les charmes de l'horreur n'enivrent que les forts!"[18] attempts to explain why a righteous superiority to tragic pleasure is so often claimed and why these experiences are shunned in literature as in life. In any case, macabre horror appeals most directly to the puritan temperament and is not common in Mexican literature.

Ghosts, on the other hand, are at home in all cultures and in all ages. The word "fantasy" itself derives from the Greek φαντασια, literally "a making visible," an apparition. The most elemental ghost story achieves its desired uncanniness simply by revealing that one of the characters is known to have died some time before we met him. The ghost may conveniently leave some object behind and thus forestall any psychological explanation of the mystery. This reliable formula is employed by Manuel Romero de Terreros in "Luna llena" (1922), Bernardo Ortiz de Montellano in "El cabo Muñoz" (1946), Carlos Toro in "La mujer azul" (1947), Felipe Montilla Duarte in "Xpet: Una visita del más allá" (1955), and by Elena Garro in "La semana de colores" (1964). The novelty of Alfredo Cardona Peña's excellent ghost story "El muro" (1966) is that there the procedure is reversed. After living for years among timid ghosts as one of them, a woman has to reveal to them that she is really alive. Cardona Peña had already found in an earlier story that inversion is an effective resource. "Más allá, también más allá" (1957) is a love story developed around a seance, but a seance that is conducted by spirits in their world. The conflict arises when they invoke a living girl and one of them falls in love with her. Francisco Tario, disinclined to employ a formula either standard or inverted, compounds the confusion of identities in "La noche de Margaret Rose" (1943), a matchless story in which the protagonist forms the terrifying conviction that the girl with whom he is playing chess is really a ghost. The light of dawn reveals, however, that she is alive but that he himself is a ghost.

The eternal themes of love and death are perfectly suited to the ghost story as is shown in many of the writings of Amado Nervo. In "La novia de Corinto" (1921), he retells a legend from ancient Greece. A young man travels to a distant city for an arranged marriage to a girl he has never met. Soon after he arrives, the girl comes to his room and introduces herself. He is pleased with her and they exchange rings. She shares some of his food and promises to return the following night. As she is leaving, her old nurse catches a glimpse of her and is astonished, for the girl, it seems, had died six months earlier. On her next visit she is intercepted and falls dead at her parents' feet. In the empty tomb they find the young man's ring. Her body is buried as a vampire beyond the city wall. In the confidential chit-chat with which Nervo frames his stories, he discredits the suggestion of vampirism and urges the reader to see only the charming story of a girl who felt lonely beyond the grave. Goethe's version of the tale, "Die Braut von Korinth" (1797), is more explicit about the vampirism; the girl there refuses the young man's food but eagerly drinks his red wine. Other variations on the corpse-bride theme in Mexican fiction occur in Guillermo Vigil y Robles's "La promesa" (1890), José Juan Tablada's "De ultratumba" (1898), and Bernardo Jiménez Montellano's "La enamorada y la muerte" (1952).

The ghost as avenging conscience is sometimes moved by personal motives as in Bernardo Couto Castillo's "Celos póstumos" (1898), but more often it has a moral purpose such as to punish disrespect for the dead (Guillermo Vigil y Robles, "La mutilada," 1890; Ciro B. Ceballos, "El guantelete," 1899; Elena Garro, "Perfecto Luna," 1958) or to avenge a murder (Manuel Romero de Terreros, "La puerta de bronce," 1922; Dr. Atl [Gerardo Murillo], "El reló del muerto," 1936; José Guadalupe Herrera Carrillo, "El extraño caso de Raimundo Díaz," 1953; Gabriel Echenique, "El Secretero," 1959).

One instance of this aggressive *deus ex machina* type of ghost story is uniquely topical. "El amo viejo" (1922) concerns an old country mansion that has been left deserted for years because of a curse. Ghostly screams and the yowling of cats are heard there by night. The owner had kept hundreds of cats on the estate just so he could mistreat them. Finally they rebelled and tore his body to pieces. The new owner proceeds to restore the mansion in defiance of the curse. Then suddenly one day the rebel *villista* troops arrive and destroy the whole estate by fire. It is perhaps ironic that the author of this allegory of class struggle, written during the Mexican Revolution, was himself an aristocrat—Don Manuel Romero de Terreros y Vinent, Marqués de San Francisco.

The fantasies of Francisco Tario are generally quite innocent. His only revenge ghost occurs in "Ave María Purísima" (1968): an angry husband returns from the grave—hopping on one foot—to punish his widow for her refusal to bury his wooden leg with him! The ominous return is described with mock horror that eventually turns to romance. The widow sustains only one injury—a love-bite on her cheek.

Tario completely disregards the established techniques of ghost-story writing. His work shows nothing of the characteristic pattern described by Peter Penzoldt:

> The ghost story deals with an unearthly and incredible manifestation in circumstances of reality. When the manifestation occurs the climax is usually reached, all the rest is exposition, a psychological preparation of the reader for the incredible events. There is no room for a plot. The whole story centers on the apparition. If the author invents a compli-

cated intrigue it will replace the apparition as the center of interest and the tale either falls to pieces or becomes that hybrid form of which one finds examples among the Gothic novels: a melodramatic narrative with a ghost among other thrilling details.[19]

In Tario's fantasy there is no incursion by the supernatural; everything is treated as quite normal. His ghosts are not agents of an angry God who desires to punish the wicked. Neither are they projections of neurotic and erotic impulses or of the evil in man's soul.

"El éxodo" (1968) relates the experiences of a family of ghosts forced into exile by the British government's 1928 decree that sought to relieve the problem of overpopulation by banishing many thousands of ghosts. A typical passage will illustrate the story's rational tone:

> Fue así que en un frío atardecer de noviembre decidí partir con mi familia, formada entonces por mi mujer y tres hijos pequeños, más una hermana de mi esposa, que más tarde habría de abandonarnos. . . . Con aguda perspicacia, todos parecíamos inclinados a emigrar hacia los países del sur, no tanto por razones de clima—esto nos tenía sin cuidado —, como porque disponíamos de información fidedigna en el sentido de que nuestra supervivencia en dichas latitudes sería más fácil y llevadera, dado que, por espacio de siglos, los naturales de aquellas regiones venían ignorando nuestra existencia y no nos importunarían en ningún caso.[20]

Nothing is illogical or distorted. The psychology of his deceptively human ghosts is well developed and their behavior perfectly consistent. Moreover, the world in which they move always seems familiar, for it is a facetious exaggeration of the observable real world.

One facet of this original author's work that should not go unobserved is the warm compassion he expresses for his creatures. In "La banca vacía" (1956), for instance, Tario expresses the thoughts of a murdered woman's ghost as she moves silently and invisibly about her home delighting in intimate reminiscence. She senses that her desired assimilation into the new state would be total if only she could die completely, but somewhere a person still remembers her and, thereby, holds her suspended. Eventually, the memory fades: "se sintió lejana y confundida, infinitamente olvidada, pero dichosa. . . . Después pensó que debería sentarse en la banca. Y así lo hizo. Pero la banca permaneció vacía."[21]

Emotion and tender sympathy also pervade "El balcón" (1957), the touching story of a mother's love for her macrocephalic child. They are always sitting together either inside their apartment or on the balcony watching the activity in the street below. The lad's delicate health and fear of being teased keep him from venturing out to play with other children. Year after year they continue their intimate relationship. But other things have changed. The building is empty of tenants: it is sealed and abandoned. The mother and child still sit on the balcony unaware that they have become ghosts. Tario makes the improbable convincing through his portrayal of their closed lives in which time had always been as if eternal. Indeed, if death is the negation of life, then they were already in death before they died.

◇◇◇◇◇◇◇◇

Tales of the supernatural form part of the oral tradition of mankind everywhere. They are told in an elementary way and rely on a few simple devices to cause in the listener a shudder in response to the uncanny nature of the events described. The supernatural presented as fact inspires a sense of fear so far as it reinforces unsurmounted doubts about the validity of the pragmatic conception of reality. The assumption of the existence of the human soul has led to the postulation of a "fourth dimension"—a separate realm inhabited by spirits. Throughout the world there are folk tales devoted to the possibility of transcending the boundary between the material domain and the spiritual. Many Mexican writers of fiction have conjectured on the nature of death (e.g., José Vasconcelos, María Elvira Bermúdez) and recounted the incursion of ghosts into the world of the living (e.g., Bernardo Ortiz de Montellano, Elena Garro) and the plight of unfortunate humans who have passed inadvertently into the other dimension (e.g., Ana de Gómez Mayorga, Amparo Dávila). In general, the literary expression of such stories in Mexico holds greater interest for the anthropologist than for the critic in search of aesthetic value. To be sure, exceptional authors such as Amado Nervo, Francisco Rojas González, and Juan de la Cabada have succeeded in creating minor works of art by their very personal and poetic use of familiar themes and motifs from popular tradition.

The idealism that prompts a writer to express himself through supernatural themes may be related to the current intellectual and social climate. Such a response, however, is only sometimes in tune with the period; at other times it represents a striking discord. Thus, although the supernatural plays a prominent role in the Romantic literature (e.g., Justo Sierra) of the anti-rationalist Reform period of Mexican history, it also abounds during the subsequent Reconstruction period when urban progress and prosperity and philosophical positivism reign triumphant. Romantic attitudes are perpetuated by the Modernists, who reject the mechanistic theory of life and affirm the importance of the spirit and of art as a way of access to truth. A surge in the frequency of supernatural themes is perceptible during certain periods (e.g., spiritualism during the Modernist period), but at no time are they totally absent from Mexican literature. Personal idealism and the human spirit are constants which, to some extent, are independent of the process of social history.

The supernatural has become a literary convention that derives mainly from European and American models. This established form is employed by certain authors (e.g., José Vasconcelos) as a vehicle for philosophical theories; whereas others (e.g., Alejandro Cuevas) consciously create Mexican content for the foreign mold, seeking thus to internationalize the culture of modern Mexico. The "cuentos macabros" of Cuevas are blatantly imitative of Poe's works, which were then so admired in Paris. Macabre tales of horror ring false in a country like Mexico where man's relation with death is so careless and familiar. More truly expressive of the Mexican attitude to the supernatural are the amusing creations of Julio Torri or Francisco Tario.

The works of Francisco Tario constitute the most original contribution by Mexican literature to the genre of the supernatural narrative. His stories, which are of undeniable human value, may be adduced to counter the repeated charge that, since fantasy implies an idealist philosophy, it can have no social or moral validity. Better than any other Mexican writer, Tario represents that "synthesis of the contradictions of reality and unreality, of reason and imagination" that the late Sir Herbert Read considered to be the true dialectic of art.[22] Tario neither offers thrills nor serves a political philosophy, but parodies life's absurdities with mild satire and a deliberate lack of seriousness. His themes are taken from popular tradition because his purpose, like that of the Romantic idealists, is to celebrate the diversity of man.

CHAPTER II

Legend and Christian Myths

Underlying every culture is a body of myths that express the cosmic view of that people. These traditional stories tell of the gods and of the creation and general nature of the universe. Myths are intimately connected with the religious beliefs and practices of the people, and are thought by many to have originated in imitation of sacred rites:

> Ritual has been, at most times and for most people, the most important thing in the world. From it have come music, dancing, painting and sculpture. All these, we have every reason to believe, were sacred long before they were secular, and the same applies to storytelling.[1]

Indeed the earliest evidence available to us indicates that literature itself seems to have begun thus, as a form of worship:

> El poderoso estado egipcio . . . , al afirmar su civilización, unos 5,000 años antes de Cristo, produjo abundante literatura conservada hasta nuestros días en textos, a la vez escritos y pintados, de papiros y piedras. . . . En el viejo Egipto existió, antes que la literatura propiamente dramática, la poesía de carácter religioso, ligada con el culto en sus manifestaciones externas: adoración de los astros, divinación de seres a la vez amados y temidos, ya que de la parte esotérica de la religión egipcia eran depositarios únicamente los sacerdotes, la minoría capacitada para seguir el curso de los astros, medir el tiempo, y predecir al campesino—el felah—cuando aumentaría el caudal del río devastador y fertilizante.[2]

The line between myth and legend is often quite vague. When

interest was first extended beyond the activities of the gods to chronicle the exploits of the larger-than-life culture heroes, the transition from myth to legend had begun. Alleged incursions of the spiritual and the divine into the affairs of men have fostered further speculation about the supernatural realm and have given rise to a multitude of legends; i.e., narratives about persons, places or events involving real or pretended belief. An essential feature of the legend is that however fantastic the material is, it is supposedly based on fact, at least insofar as the teller of the tale is concerned.

A. LEGEND

Originally the term legend (Latin, *legenda*) was applied to readings for Christian devotion: accounts of the lives and miracles of the saints to be read at religious service or at meals. Mexican literature abounds in stories of the miracles performed by saints and priests, images and crosses. The folk tales of the people become the traditions of the Church; what began as pious invention comes to be regarded as a manifestation of the Holy Spirit.

The legend of Mexico's protomartyr and saint Felipe de Jesús (1573–1597) is related by Luis Malo in *Vida del diablo* (1876) and again by Vicente Riva Palacio in "La leyenda de un santo" (1893). As a boy, Felipe was very mischievous and his mother would often exclaim in exasperation, "¡Felipe, Dios te haga un santo!" meaning perhaps that only thus would he reach heaven.[3] Their black maid would always scoff and say to herself "¿Felipillo santo? Cuando la higuera reverdezca."[4] One morning in winter years later the maid looks in astonishment at the dead fig tree to which she has so often referred, whereupon she runs into the house shouting "¡Señora, señora! ¡Felipillo santo! ¡Felipillo santo! ¡La higuera ha reverdecido!"[5] According to tradition, the miracle occurred on the very day (Feb. 13, 1597) when Felipe was crucified along with other missionaries in Nagasaki, Japan. Fernando Benítez explains the importance of Felipe de Jesús in Mexican culture as follows:

> Like Cuauhtémoc, our greatest lay hero, this hero of the Church represents a denouement. A far from common martyrdom plucked him from anonymity and granted him admission to the exalted company he now enjoys in heaven. He is a Mexican, a Creole, a native of the city, and the patron saint of silversmiths, the aristocrat of the national guilds. He has been beloved by the devout for centuries because he was young, handsome, of the same nationality as they, and because he behaved in foreign lands like the best of the saints. He is the invention of a people in need of affirmations, and they do not call him merely Saint Felipe, but by the pet name of Felipillo Santo; they weave legends around him and

deck him in a garment of hopes and dreams despite the efforts of his biographers to strip him of it.[6]

In "Las flores del pino" (1938) Artemio de Valle-Arizpe has recorded a legend that is essentially a variation of the reviving tree motif. Catalina García del Real is in love with Don Rafael Rivadesella, who leads her to believe that eventually he will marry her. Fifteen years pass and still Don Rafael has not proposed marriage. In the meantime, Catalina's parents have died and her future is uncertain. When Fray Antonio de Yepes, the respected superior of the convent of San Francisco, confronts Don Rafael and demands clarification of his intentions, the latter replies impertinently that he will marry Catalina, but only when the pine tree by his house bears flowers. The next day Don Rafael finds his pine covered with large, red, rose-like blossoms.

Artemio de Valle-Arizpe has also provided Mexican literature with a counterpart of the familiar Peruvian *tradición*, "El alacrán de Fray Gómez." In characteristically simple, ironic style, Ricardo Palma recorded the miracles performed by Fray Gómez. In particular, he told how the saintly friar helped a poor devout peddler by lending him a scorpion to pawn. The creature was miraculously transformed into a precious jewel until redeemed and brought back to Fray Gómez. Supposedly historical details about the central figure—his birth in Extremadura in 1560; entry into the Franciscan order in 1580; arrival in Lima in 1587; and his death on May 2, 1631—help to persuade the reader that there is some truth to this story, first published in Palma's *Ropa vieja* (Lima: Imprenta del Universo, de Carlos Prince, 1889). As retold by Artemio de Valle-Arizpe, the legend is set in Mexico and named "El alacrán de Fray Anselmo" (1931). The saint is now Fray Anselmo de Medina and the supplicant Don Lorenzo Baena, a prominent merchant who is ruined when his shipments of goods are assaulted by pirates and bandits. Valle-Arizpe's narrative is more developed, more conventional and impersonal than that of Palma, yet both tell essentially the same story. At the conclusion Fray Gómez addressed the scorpion with the words "Animalito de Dios, sigue tu camino"; the Mexican Fray Anselmo de Medina says, "Anda, sigue tu camino, criaturita de Dios." Valle-Arizpe was doubtless familiar with the works of Ricardo Palma but, given the ease with which folk tales become widely disseminated, it can be assumed that he based his story on local Mexican tradition.[7]

Eerie tales of the supernatural and of saintly miracles have their common source in fear and Christian morality. Both are essentially tales of the marvelous that appeal directly to the unconscious and reinforce the simple animistic beliefs with which man has sought to explain the universe by casting himself as beneficiary of the spiritual struggle between good and evil being waged in a realm unseen but intensely real.

The theme of the pathetic soul condemned for his sins to live on in torment after death has always been popular in Mexico. One of the oldest and most generally attested legends is that of the *Llorona*, the wailing woman. She has been reported in all parts of Mexico and indeed throughout Latin America and beyond. Usually she appears on stormy nights, dressed in white robes and lamenting "Ay, mis hijos." Any number of versions of her identity and the nature of her sin exist among the people. Many say she is Doña Marina, known as *la Malinche*, who suffers eternal torment for the betrayal of her people to the Spanish invaders. Other accounts are given in stories by Ramón Rodríguez Rivera, "La Llorona: cuento popular" (1883); Luis González Obregón, "La Llorona" (1922); and Dr. Atl, "El aullido de la Llorona" (1941).[8] Rodríguez Rivera claims that she was a woman from his state of Veracruz, who murdered her baby and her husband during a fit of unfounded jealousy. The learned Franciscan Friar Bernardino de Sahagún identifies the *Llorona* with the earth goddess Cihuacóatl (Serpent Woman), sometimes called Tonántzin (Our Mother). In his *Historia general de las cosas de Nueva España* he records that she

> aparecía muchas veces, según dicen, como una señora compuesta con unos atavíos como se usan en palacio. Decían que de noche voceaba y bramaba en el aire. . . . Los atavíos con que esta mujer aparecía eran blancos, y los cabellos los tocaba de manera que tenía como unos cornezuelos cruzados sobre la frente.[9]

Moreover, of the many omens foretelling the coming of the Spaniards, the sixth was

> que se oyó de noche en el aire una voz de una mujer que decía: ¡Oh hijos míos, ya nos perdimos!; algunas veces decía: ¡Oh hijos míos, adónde os llevaré![10]

The true origin of the *Llorona* may never be satisfactorily established, although in a recent study Robert A. Barakat has taken Mexican and Brazilian versions of the legend and has attempted to link them with the Sirens of Greek mythology.[11]

The soul in torment manifests itself in order to excite pity in the witness, who may be asked specifically to undertake a certain penance or to arrange a number of special masses in order to hasten the soul's passage through Purgatory. Carlos Sigüenza y Góngora related one such story—the earliest account of a legend in Mexican literature —in his *Paraíso occidental*.[12] Luis González Obregón repeated it as "Lo que aconteció a una monja con un clérigo difunto: leyenda de la Calle de Jesús María" (1922) and Artemio de Valle-Arizpe as "La marca de fuego" (1932). In many other legends the grateful soul reveals the location of a buried treasure—an immediate and tangible reward for virtue, which, naturally, has a strong appeal.

Among the legends Gregorio Torres Quintero relates of his native Colima is "El sueño del pobre y del rico" (1931), in which a poor shoemaker buys a haunted house so that he might meet a ghost that could make him rich. A ghost does appear to him in a dream. It tells him to go from Sayula to Zapotlán and there to seek out a wealthy merchant named Manzano. In Zapotlán, Manzano offers the shoemaker nothing but does tell him of a dream he had about a treasure buried between two peach trees beside a well. The shoemaker recognizes the description of his own property, returns home to Sayula and uncovers the treasure. Torres Quintero may have found this story in Colima, as he says, but it had already appeared elsewhere. In the *Arabian Nights' Entertainments*, the tale corresponding to the 351st and 352nd Nights is called "The Ruined Man who Became Rich Again Through a Dream," and relates how an impoverished merchant of Baghdad is told in a dream that in Cairo he will find his fortune. He makes the long journey to Cairo, but there he is mistaken for a criminal and imprisoned. When he tells his story, the Wali, or Chief of Police, calls him a fool for acting on a dream. It seems the Wali also had had a dream but he was too wise to heed it. In his dream, a voice said,

> . . . there is in Baghdad a house in such a district and of such a fashion and its courtyard is laid out garden-wise, at the lower end whereof is a jetting-fountain and under the same a great sum of money lieth buried. Go thither and take it.[13]

The merchant returned to his home and uncovered the money.

The example of the *Llorona* illustrated the common phenomenon of a legend that is shared by several countries. "La Mulata de Córdoba" is another legend firmly rooted in Mexican tradition, but which also figures prominently in the heritage of another country, Guatemala. Numerous Mexican authors, including Luis Malo, José Bernardo Couto, Luis González Obregón, and José Pérez Moreno, have recorded how this beautiful woman, reputedly from Córdoba, Veracruz, escaped being burned as a witch by sailing away in a ship that she had sketched with charcoal on the wall of her prison cell. Guatemalans know the story as the "Leyenda de la Tatuana." Miguel Ángel Asturias depicts the *Tatuana* as an innocent slave-girl thought to be possessed by a devil.[14] A kindly priest uses his fingernail to scratch a tattoo of a ship on her arm and informs her that she can escape anytime by drawing a similar picture on a wall. Asturias suggests that the name *Tatuana* probably began as *Tatuada* and that it alludes to a tattoo's magical ability to render the bearer invisible. In another Guatemalan version, Francisco Barnoya Gálvez shows her as an authentic witch who arrived in the Captaincy General of Guatemala by the same marvelous ship in which she was to escape from the Inquisition.[15]

All legends are thought to have some basis in fact. Yet seldom has the intimate relation between historical fact and popular legend been so clearly demonstrated as in the case of the tradition arising from certain events that occurred in the street formerly known as the Calle de Olmedo in the center of Mexico City. From the popular tradition, José María Roa Bárcena created his delightful story "Lanchitas" (1877), set in the year 1820 or 1830. Padre Lanzas, affectionately known as Lanchitas, is accosted on the street one evening by an old woman who implores him to accompany her, for someone urgently requires confession. In a distant house, he is shown a gaunt, sickly youth, who obviously is dying. The youth claims that years earlier he had died in violent circumstances and had been unable to confess his sins. Lanchitas, who is not alarmed since he is accustomed to dealing with demented people, hears the confession and grants absolution. Later that night he relates the incident to some friends, one of whom happens to be the owner of the particular house Lanchitas describes. He swears it has been empty and locked for years. When they investigate they find the door covered with cobwebs and the lock rusted solid. But inside they find Lanchita's handkerchief and eventually a skeleton is discovered within the wall. The shock of having confessed a ghost drives Lanchitas insane.

By the time Vicente Riva Palacio versified the legend, twenty-three years later, several details had become altered.[16] The year was fixed as 1731, the priest's name was Fray Mendo, the person requiring confession was a beautiful girl, the article Fray Mendo left behind was his rosary, and the shock of discovery killed him.

Early in this century Luis González Obregón uncovered documents in the Archivo General de la Nación that established the facts on which the legend was founded.[17] A priest named D. Juan Antonio Nuño Vázquez actually registered an official complaint that at eight o'clock on the night of September 15, 1791, he was taken forcibly, tied and blindfolded, to a place where he heard the confessions of two people, a man and a woman. He was found late that night near the Casa de Moneda. The priest had no idea of the location of the house and he refused to divulge the nature of the confessions he had been forced to hear. Documents are preserved of the futile investigation made by the authorities, which was initiated by the Viceroy himself. Here, then, is a striking illustration of legend conceived of as "unauthenticated narrative, folk-embroidered from historical materials.''[18]

B. CHRISTIAN MYTHS

Speculative supernatural fiction deriving from folk tradition is often of limited artistic value when the author is primarily interested in convincing the reader of the authenticity of the marvelous central element which erupts into his normal world. The theme of commerce between the natural and the supernatural worlds offends the intellectual faculties of many modern readers, which effectively prevents them from appreciating this type of fiction. A purer kind of fantasy frankly approaching the poetic fairy tale arouses less intellectual opposition.

In pure fantasy, the author takes possession of the physical world and transfers it to the spiritual realm: he invents an autonomous world from the common perceptions and conceptions of everyday reality, which he arbitrarily recombines for his own purpose. Fantasy, this product of the poet's fancy, can be pure diversion or it can be charged with critical intent. In either case, the response sought is not merely the uncanny shiver, but also aesthetic or recreational enjoyment, together with an incidental heightened awareness of reality.

After Mexico achieved Independence, many writers began to look back with nostalgia to the comparatively stable colonial period. Like Spain's Romantics, they described past customs and legends with more emphasis on Christian idealism than on the quality of their prose. In the twentieth century, a resurgence of interest in the past accompanied the Mexican Revolution. Consideration of national subjects was prompted also by the First World War, which isolated the Mexican writer from his customary European sources of inspiration. The *colonialistas* sought above all to escape from the turmoil of the revolution, but in their work they professed a faith in their Spanish heritage and deplored Frenchified *modernista* literature. They believed, moreover, that better understanding of the past might cast light on the current political and social crisis. More often antiquarians than poets, most of them cultivated the well-documented and polished but sterile and static kind of legend in which Artemio de Valle-Arizpe alone persevered until his death in 1961.

There were a few among the *colonialistas*, though, who took standard motifs from folk tradition and employed them solely for their aesthetic value. One of the best of the invented ''literary legends''—notable more for their exquisite style than for their content—is Jorge de Godoy's ''El puñado de rubíes'' (1921), in which a fierce bandit prevents his men from assaulting a woman and her child, but is badly wounded in the struggle. The child lays its hand on the bloody wound and miraculously the pain ceases. On the following day a priest in a nearby church is astonished to find that the garments on the image of the Virgin are stained with mud, and in the hand of the child Jesus is a string of rubies. Jorge de Godoy has transformed a standard miracle tale into a poem of lyrical, harmonious prose. The whole of nature is alive—the birds and animals converse, the forest spirits convene—in a fairy tale atmosphere that makes the miracle perfectly acceptable.

In "Un salteador" (1936), a beautiful if sentimental tale by Francisco Monterde, we have another highwayman. This one is waiting alone by a mountain road on a cold winter's night. It is the eve of the *Día de Reyes* and the poor man's children will find no gifts in their shoes next morning unless he can rob someone. Eventually, an old man comes along the road. The highwayman takes his purse and lets him go. Then in quick succession two more men arrive and are handily robbed. The purses, labeled Melchor, Gaspar and Baltasar, contain gold coins, toys, and sweets. The highwayman thinks of how happy his children will be, but when he tries to set out for home he discovers that he cannot move. In the morning his frozen body is discovered.

Western man owes a great deal of his intellectual formation and his personal psychology to the myths of Christianity, insofar as they determined the culture into which he was born. These myths are as much a part of his reality as is the physical world. On the one hand, there is religious belief, which solemnly admits, for instance, the physical ascent of a saint to heaven; on the other is common experienced reality, subject as it is to natural laws. Convention recommends that both views be held simultaneously, and makes no allowance for capricious variations. Enrique Anderson Imbert, himself a writer of fantasy, has discussed the relationship between literary fantasy and religion as follows:

> Todo el mundo sabe que lo insoportable del teólogo es su falta de imaginación. Ni siquiera puede imaginar la inexistencia de Dios. . . . Estoy persuadido de que si surgiera una gran literatura fantástica con temas católicos, sería una literatura descreída, porque un tema religioso se hace poesía cuando es invención, no cuando es creencia. El día que los ángeles parezcan tan bellos como las hadas será porque la gente ha dejado de creer que son mensajeros de un Dios verdadero.[19]

Two important characteristics of the revolutionary period—ardent nationalism and religious skepticism—are joined by Mariano Silva y Aceves in "Las rosas de Juan Diego" (1916). From Mexico's most sacred legend, that of the Virgin of Guadalupe, this classical scholar has created an admirable poem in prose. In his version, Silva y Aceves maliciously portrays the simple Indian Juan Diego as a naive idiot, despised and mocked by everyone. The girls, in particular, seek to take advantage of him:

> En las recién casadas, la gracia de Juan Diego despertaba deseos pecaminosos y aun se supo de alguna que se atrevió a provocar aquella inocencia, en ocasión propicia, allá en la quiebra de la montaña; mas Juan Diego, lejos de interesarse, corrió a contar el suceso a los viandantes, llamándoles a socorrer a aquella mujer que le parecía víctima de un doloroso accidente.[20]

Juan Diego does not welcome the Virgin's appearance because she cuts some of his beloved mountain roses and, moreover, she too wants to seduce him away from his state of innocence: "Y si quieres, Juan Diego, . . . vivirás conmigo y tendrás siempre las mejores rosas del valle. Yo soy la diosa de los rosales y te daré los que quieras a condición de que vivas en mi huerto; . . . en mi huerto serás dueño y tendremos los dos nuestro deseo."[21] Silva y Aceves gives forewarning of his irreverent treatment by choosing the epigraph

> —Femme, qui est tu?
> —Je suis la vierge Orberose.

from Anatole France, another master of elegant irony.[22]

A cynical view of religion in Mexico is offered by Armando Olivares in "La ofrenda" (1954). Saint Anne comes to earth, eager to serve God's children, and takes up residence in an ugly plaster image of herself in a humble village church. Her miracles attract an opportunistic priest and such a horde of greedy pilgrims that Saint Anne returns to Heaven in disgust. Once the miracles cease, the worshippers again abandon the little church. Before long the doors are smashed for firewood and the lifeless image is stolen.

Curiously, Jesus himself seldom appears as a character in Mexican fantasy. Salvador Calvillo Madrigal's story "El Señor Aquél" (1959) is one remarkably flippant portrayal of the Lord. His identity is suggested by the capital letters of the title and is confirmed by details such as the stigmata on his hands. One morning on Mexico City's Avenida Juárez, the narrator meets a crabbed old man with a roll of newspapers under his arm. They had met once before, years earlier, by the lake in Chapultepec Park, but the old man is greatly changed. Formerly serene and confident, he has become sullen and discouraged. His matted beard, ragged suit, and broken shoes give him the appearance of a "Carlos Marx en la miseria."[23] Señor Aquél confirms the impious tone of the story as he accepts the offer of a cup of coffee:

—Un café—repuso tras de instantánea vacilación—no es cosa de rechazar. Efectivamente cae muy bien a cualquier hora. Y siempre es mucho mejor que el vinagre. Una vez me hicieron tragar vinagre; desde entonces quedé un poco delicado del estómago.[24]

At the sound of a newsboy who enters the restaurant shouting the day's headlines, Señor Aquél pounds on the table and begins a tirade against the state of the world. He points furiously at the abundant evidence of stupidity, hatred and violence recorded in the newspapers. Enraged, he leaves the restaurant, crosses the Alameda and enters the Iglesia de San Juan de Dios. The narrator observes, finally, "Que al penetrar no se quitó el sombrero. Parecía que entraba en su propia casa."[25]

Angels "tan bellos como las hadas"[26] such as Anderson Imbert recommends already do occur in Mexican literature, notably in the works of Amado Nervo. The subtitle of "El 'ángel caído' " (1921)— (Cuento de Navidad, dedicado a mi sobrina, María de los Ángeles)— and the opening sentence—"Érase un ángel que, por retozar más de la cuenta sobre una nube crepuscular teñida de violetas, perdió pie y cayó lastimosamente a la tierra"[27]—clearly indicate what sort of story it will be. The little angel injures a wing and is cared for lovingly by a humble Mexican family. The children and the angel play together and when he is better the angel takes them flying. Eventually, when he has to return to heaven, the children beg him to take them and he complies. Later he returns for their mother. In another of Nervo's Christmas stories, "Como en las estampas" (1921), an angel persuades God to reconstruct heaven temporarily to conform to the picture-book ideal held by a delicate young girl who is soon to arrive. Other sentimental stories of fair angels bearing children up to heaven are "La parábola del niño pobre" (1942) by Luis Mendieta y Núñez and "El ángel" (1964) by Rubén Marín.

Admission into heaven is rather more difficult for an adult than for an innocent child. The adult's actions and motives must all be reviewed and measured against a rigorous standard. María Elvira Bermúdez has written two stories ("En el umbral de la Gloria" [1955] and "Lo que atares en la tierra. . ." [1966]) protesting against the arbitrary restriction of free thought. With compassion and extraordinary technical skill, Bermúdez develops hypothetical situations to demonstrate how the technicalities of Christian dogma, if strictly observed, can lead to inhumane and absurd conclusions. It is an individual's adherence to the code of behavior prescribed by society that determines his advancement during life—and afterwards as well.

"Quedito, el afortunado" (1954) by Armando Olivares is a parable that deplores the rewards of hypocrisy. The protagonist manages, by assuming a posture of extreme humility, to arouse feelings of pity in his associates and superiors. All obstacles are withdrawn from his path as he coasts easily through his political career. Death, too, is gentle with him and St. Peter at the gates of heaven cannot bear to turn him back. Once he is safely inside, he drops his modesty like a mask and, inflated with arrogant pride, settles down to enjoy Eternity.[28] Olivares fails to indicate what kind of enjoyment is to be found there.

St. Peter can be deceived, it seems, but he can not be intimidated by the wealthy and influential. The Mexican newspaper magnate and millionaire José García Valseca is lampooned by Daniel Cadena in two vitriolic novels, . . .*por el ojo de la aguja*. . . (1961) and *La aguja en el pajar* (1962), which describe the vain attempts of his wicked soul to force entry into heaven. The novels contain preliminary statements addressed to the Señores Ministros de la Cuarta Sala de la Suprema Corte de Justicia de la Nación, in which Cadena swears that García Valseca had dismissed him from his newspaper and by chicanery had avoided paying any compensation for his twenty-two years of service. Cadena's legal suit finally came before the Supreme Court of the Nation after six years of litigation. A curious precedent was estab- lished, as the Supreme Court allowed Cadena to submit the two fanciful novels as his formal allegation. It is even more surprising because of the potentially libelous character of the works, which accuse García Valseca by name of having committed numerous spe- cific crimes and of having threatened to murder Cadena if he persisted in the lawsuit. Unfortunately, the sardonic tone of these fantasies and the constant personal invective make it impossible for the reader to disregard the real background and enjoy the charm implicit in the setting and plot. It must be noted, in passing, that the Supreme Court ruled in favor of the plaintiff Daniel Cadena.

Dr. Atl's comic novel *El Padre Eterno, Satanás y Juanito García* (1938), in contrast, succeeds despite personal attacks on his contem- poraries, as they are only incidental and have no function beyond his facetious treatment of world politics and religions. Indiscriminately, he derides José Vasconcelos, Woodrow Wilson, Michael (the arch- angel), Pancho Villa, Jehovah, Trotsky, Clemenceau, and General Foch. As with all utopian fiction, descriptions of heaven are intended primarily to convey their author's ideas about his own world. Even though it is indirect, the satire is unmistakable when Dr. Atl has God test a new form of government with Gabriel as leader of the Partido Nacional Revolucionario Celestial Pro Regeneración Humana (P.N.R.C.P.R.H.)[29] or when Manuel Balbontín, in *Memorias de un muerto* (1874), introduces a Martian visitor in heaven to describe the social injustices on his planet. José Ferrel's amusing story "Un viaje al Cielo" (1898) constitutes a bold criticism of *diazpotismo* in its outline of celestial politics. It shows, for instance, how the Divino Dictador artfully checks unrest within his government by such measures as the unlikely appointment of Death to the post of Ministro de la Vida. Evidence of political corruption is provided in the example of St. Peter,

> que era Portero del Cielo, es ahora Secretario particular del Ministro de la Vida. Parece que buenas influencias lo han elevado a tal cargo. Empieza a murmurarse de que los negocios públicos se atienden con mucha calma y de que el Soberano se está dejando dominar por los Ministros de Mejoras Celestes, que ya llevan mucho tiempo en el poder, falseando así las Leyes Divinas que rigen los espacios.[30]

The Mexican public reading this story in 1898 could not have failed to associate it with the regime of Porfirio Díaz, who, by altering the Constitution and holding mock elections, had already succeeded himself as President in 1888, 1892, and 1896. Furthermore, the constant shifting of officials was a characteristic feature of the *Porfiriato*. John Edwin Fagg has described it as "a perpetual game of juggling personalities—of cabinet ministers, generals, state governors, police officers, and congressmen; Díaz played it with unparalleled cunning."[31] This shrewd manipulation served to keep the officials responsible solely and directly to Díaz himself and to prevent the formulation of small alliances which could threaten the dictator's power.

Such satirical undercurrents are probably necessary to hold our interest in guided tours of heaven, for the angelic inhabitants by themselves are unavoidably dull. The Devil and his apostate angels of hell are more akin to our imperfect nature; hence, they seem to us more believable as characters in fiction. Moreover, they bring that necessary element of evil without which there can be no conflict and no story.

We are mildly interested by power struggles among the demons —as in Vicente Riva Palacio's "La horma de su zapato" (1893)—but it is the struggle between the Devil and man that enthralls us. The ever-popular theme of a pact with the Devil has often been employed in Mexican literature, but with undistinguished results, except in two cases: Diego Cañedo's "Vida, expiación y muerte de Arístides Elorrio" (1956) and Juan José Arreola's early and untypically idealistic "Un pacto con el diablo" (1943). Cañedo's story is notable for its ingenuity and polished style; Arreola's for its accomplished inner structure.

In general, Maximilian Rudwin is correct in his observation that "each generation and each nation has a special and distinct devil related to its own temperament."[32] Yet anachronistic portrayals of Satan will occur because the writer's personal conception of evil may differ appreciably from that held by society. Dr. Luis Malo reveals a medieval conception of Satan in *Vida del diablo* (1876), a tiresome series of biographical anecdotes from biblical and traditional sources. Each is related to the author's own time to illustrate the continuing presence of evil in the world. Malo, who identifies himself as a priest, is very insistent, for example, about the evil influence of all women since Eve, and predictably he attributes diabolic inspiration to Benito Juárez, whose Reform Laws fettered the Church.

The personification of evil once was immediately recognizable by his tail and cloven hoofs, his costume, and an odor of sulphur. Today he is likely to be anonymous or simply an abstraction whose presence can only be inferred from the dramatic action. A devil in Alfonso Reyes's mock-sinister "Encuentro con un diablo" (1959) reveals his identity only after suspicions are aroused by his heretical statements. In "La desilusión del diablo" (1949), Carlos Villamil Castillo pictures a very human devil. This dejected figure has come to a baseball park to find someone who will listen to his complaints about how nowadays no one fears or respects him. The unclear notion of evil itself in our age of relativistic morality is reflected in the mutual contamination among angels and devils in Alfredo Cardona Peña's "Origen de la nostalgia" (1966) and "El mejor cuento de misterio" (1962), together with its "Epílogo. . ." (1966).

Despite the number of Mexican writers who have employed the myths proposed by Christianity to explain the origin and purpose of creation, it is remarkable how few have been satisfied to exploit the essential poetry of these myths. In many cases, they have taken myth merely as a conventional vehicle for an ideological pronouncement. An extreme example of the unfortunate use of fantasy is *La rebelión de Satán* (1945?). Here J. F. Vereo Guzmán presents his version of world history, which is designed to show how utterly Christianity has failed against the corruption of wealth, colonialism and property. This hysterical novel culminates in the communist revelation and closes with the triumphant cry "¡EL NUEVO JESUCRISTO ES EL TRA-BAJO!"[33] Similarly, Dr. Atl uses *El Padre Eterno, Satanás y Juanito García* to destroy God and proclaim his absolute faith in the redemptive power of science. Such partisan distortions of Christian cosmogony divest the myths of their real human value just as art is depreciated when placed at the service of an extraneous objective ideal. Fanciful variations of myths are more satisfactory when they seek only to entertain. Such a case is "Alegoría presuntuosa" (1953) by María Elvira Bermúdez, in which a complex psychological drama arises from the relations between Equis the creator, his opponent Anti-Equis, and the creatures Minus and Mina. Bermúdez does, in fact, suggest deep and futile motives for the creation, but the story's impulse is more frivolous than philosophical.

◇◇◇◇◇◇◇◇

No longer do legends commonly appear in literary form in Mexico, although they still survive in oral tradition. Even when legends were eagerly collected and refined for publication, that is, during the nineteenth century (José Justo Gómez de la Cortina, José María Roa Bárcena, Vicente Riva Palacio) and early in the twentieth century (Luis González Obregón, Manuel Romero de Terreros, Artemio de Valle-Arizpe), they always showed a trace of nostalgia, as if longing for the naive innocence of some earlier age:

> La leyenda es la flor de la admiración que el pueblo ofrenda a lo sublime. La leyenda es la expresión más delicada de la literatura popular. El mundo, en las leyendas, quiere evadirse de la vulgaridad cotidiana, embelleciendo la prosa de la vida con una soñada espiritualidad.
>
> El pueblo siente y ríe en otros géneros, adoctrinándose con la experiencia o deleitándose con su gracia; pero la leyenda guarda lo más fino de sus esencias y lo más delicado de su emoción. Las viejas leyendas son lecciones íntimas de la antigüedad, como espejo del pensamiento de un mundo que se fue, sencillo, cordial y creyente.[34]

Popular legends are handed down by tradition as unverified but generally believed stories about specific persons and events. This notwithstanding, they are capable of crossing linguistic, cultural, and historical boundaries (e.g. la Llorona, la Mulata de Córdoba), and in each new setting their local origin is affirmed with conviction. Such legends are of value for their ingenuous charm and as folk expression that embodies some aspect of the national character.

During the turbulent years 1915–1923, a group of Mexican writers dedicated themselves to creating a new form of literature which combined elements of the legend with elements of the short story. Their work found its inspiration in the national past, particularly in the daily life of New Spain; hence it came to be known as colonialismo or virreinalismo. Luis González Obregón, primarily a scholar, sought to throw light on the fragments of history that had been carried along in popular legends. Artemio de Valle-Arizpe was the most prolific of those authors who emulated Ricardo Palma and attempted to resurrect the glory of Spain in America by piecing together material discovered in old documents and in popular tradition. They wrote in a baroque, graceful but archaic style suited to the portrayal of a baroque period of history, but they never attained the charm that characterizes the work of Ricardo Palma. Other members of the *colonialista* group (e.g. Jorge de Godoy and Francisco Monterde) were not interested in what was circumstantial and factual in the legends; they celebrated only the essential beauty and poetry. Their folk-inspired stories are personal works of art, not historical reconstructions.

Unlike legends, the familiar myths of Christianity continue to provide a basis for literature in modern Mexico. The legends were narrated in a pious and sober tone as objects of belief, although their connection with historical fact was seldom demonstrable. Myths, in contrast, refer to a world supposed to have preceded the present order, a time so remote that they are easily regarded as symbolic and thus can be freely adapted by the writer's fancy. Mexican variations on themes from Christian mythology—angels and devils, heaven and hell—are usually cast in the form of short stories, sometimes poetic, sometimes humorous, ironic, and satirical.

CHAPTER III ---

Literary Divertissements

Literature as pure play is little cultivated in Mexico, where art is generally seen as an instrument for social progress.[1] Nevertheless, there are authors, often inspired by foreign literatures, who flout convention and indulge their fancy in capricious inventions that may have nothing to do with the national culture or mythology. Such writings do not seek to convey insights into the nature of reality (as does literature of the imagination), but merely offer brief escape. The elements of common reality become poetized as they are arbitrarily recombined for fun and aesthetic enjoyment. The idea that this is precisely what literature should be finds little support among Spanish-American theorists. A notable exception, Enrique Anderson Imbert declares the purpose of art to be the transformation of all reality—physical and psychic—into symbols:

> En el fondo [la literatura] es un esfuerzo para liberarse de la realidad, tanto de la física, que nos oprime desde fuera, como de la psíquica, que nos inunda con un turbión de sentimientos, impulsos e ideas. El poeta (llamemos así para abreviar, a todos los creadores de literatura) se autocontempla; y al autocontemplarse descubre que ciertas experiencias muy personales le producen una peculiar fruición estética. Lo que le interesa, en tanto poeta, no es la realidad, sino esa imagen estéticamente valiosa que acaba de descubrirse en el espejo de su conciencia. A la realidad el poeta la puso a distancia. Al distanciarla, la realidad dejó un hueco. Y es en este hueco donde se ha aparecido un simulacro envuelto en símbolos artísticos.[2]

Pedro Henríquez Ureña, on the other hand, conceived of art as

following two paths—one serious and important, the other of
doubtful value:

> El arte había obedecido hasta ahora a dos fines humanos: uno, la ex-
> presión de los anhelos profundos, del ansia de eternidad, del utópico y
> siempre renovado sueño de la vida perfecta; otro, el juego, el solaz
> imaginativo en que descansa el espíritu. El arte y la literatura de nues-
> tros días [1926] apenas recuerdan ya su antigua función trascendental;
> sólo nos va quedando el juego. . . . Y el arte reducido a diversión
> inteligente, pirotecnia del ingenio, acaba en hastío.[3]

The *jeu d'esprit* is but one of many types of literary fantasy and is such
an easy target that it is regularly selected for attack by critics who
require realistic transcriptions of the world. Unfortunately, the dis-
credit is extended indiscriminately to other types of fantasy and even
to literature of the imagination. Henríquez Ureña's observation, however, concerns the general neglect of the more transcendent art and
does not really deplore the mere existence of fantasy.

Francisco Tario is Mexico's boldest author of sustained invention. His caprices are intended simply for enjoyment and lay
claim to no more intrinsic importance than do fairy tales. Tario
proceeds by arbitrarily suspending certain of nature's laws and then
carrying the whimsical idea to its limit, or else he exaggerates a
common attitude in order to laugh at the human condition or lampoon solemn aspects of life. The title-character of "El mico" (1968) is
a miniature person born of a water faucet into a contented bachelor's
apartment. The tiny creature arouses maternal emotions in the young
man, who soon becomes its willing slave. When finally the role
becomes intolerable he returns the *mico* to its place of origin, flushing
it down the toilet. From this gentle satire of motherhood and house-
wifery, Tario turns to yet another social institution—the private concern of the father as pivot of all family life. The father in the story
"Ortodoncia" (1968) is so absurdly obsessed with his dental problem
that he is rather a figure of derision than of respect within the family.
The climax occurs when he attempts to crack a filbert with his only
tooth. He appears to succeed, but later the tooth falls out and he
commits suicide.

The product of fancy is often slight and elemental—more a sustained metaphor or poetic conceit than a narrative. Tario's personification of musical forms, for instance, in "La noche del vals y el
nocturno" (1943) is pure whimsy; the love affair between two books of
music in Rafael Solana's "El concerto" (1943) merely serves, like the
subplot of a Golden Age drama, to parallel the main action. Mild
amusement is provided by the unusual point of view in Leopoldo
Sánchez Zúber's "La rendija" (1966)—an examination of the motives

of a seam opening in a lady's tight dress to free the imprisoned flesh—
and by Alfredo Cardona Peña's "Un cuadro en la Eternidad" (1966), in
which he imagines what might happen if Velásquez were to stop
painting *Las meninas* and step out of the picture briefly to rest his
arm. An element of self-mockery is apparent in "La broca" (1960), a
trivial piece by María Luisa Hidalgo, which depicts an insect larva or
bookworm proud of her learning and a great expert on rare editions.

Such light-weight, inconsequential inventions provide many
readers with welcome distraction from dull or miserable circumstances. Escapism is discouraged in an age of science; yet man still
has a spiritual need for beauty and he must sustain his sense of
wonder. It was in this complementary capacity that Amado Nervo
understood the necessity of art:

> Nosotros, hombres serios de este orto del siglo XX; nosotros, hombres
> desdeñosos del prodigio, atiborrados de filosofía positiva, orgullosos
> de la linternita temblorosa con que alumbramos un pie cuadrado de
> terreno en medio de este océano sin límites de lo desconocido ... ;
> nosotros nos perecemos por el milagro, por los cuentos de nodriza,
> exactamente como nuestros antepasados. Sólo que, temerosos de que
> padezca nuestra infantil reputación de hombres de seso, de personas
> formales, en el día hacemos la comedia de la seriedad, y en la noche
> sacamos de debajo de la almohada el libro que nos transporta a mundos
> desconocidos.[4]

Narrative equivalents of the sentimental lyric occur often in the
works of Manuel Gutiérrez Nájera—an example is his delightful "Los
amores del cometa" (1882)—and in those of many other nineteenth-
century authors. In Julio Torri's fine prose poem or parable "La balada
de las hojas más altas" (1917), we overhear leaves (artists?) as they
discuss a medieval caravan (life?) that is passing along the dusty road
below. From their lofty private domain they express pity for worldly
mortals who miss nature's subtle, exquisite beauty because they are
caught up in the ugliness of everyday reality. These and pretty compositions like "El mosquito Patas Largas"(1946), in which Héctor
Morales Saviñón relates the tragic love idyll of a mosquito and a
coquettish butterfly, derive from the French theory of *l'art pour l'art*
and ultimately from Poe's "The Poetic Principle" (1850): There neither exists nor *can* exist any work more thoroughly dignified ... than
... this poem written solely for the poem's sake."[5]

The device of personification is not necessarily gratuitous or
employed for its aesthetic value alone. It often serves to poke fun at a
human foible. Pride of ancestry is satirized by Morales Saviñón in
"Las angustias del coco" (1946). The arrogance of a cocoanut, who
boasts vainly of a distinguished ancestor who killed an Englishman

by landing on his head, is humbled when an American tourist orders it cut down after buying it for "guan peso." The American drains it and throws it into the sea, where the waves pound it against the sand until it becomes soft and repentant. In another case—"La decepción de la pulga" (1949) by Carlos Villamil Castillo—a flea of aristocratic birth expresses the opinion that human behavior is even more disgusting than that of dogs.

One form of narrative that was especially popular in the nineteenth century is the autobiographical account of the adventures of a common inanimate object. Essentially variations of the picaresque tradition, these episodic satires present a gallery of human types in the successive owners of the object.

A talking coin appears as the central character in stories by José Joaquín Pesado, José Bernardo Couto, and Manuel Gutiérrez Nájera. In "La historia de un peso" (1882), Couto directs mild criticism against doctors, priests, landlords, idlers, and merchants alike; but when he attacks corrupt public officials, taking instances of bribery in the Customs Service and in the Courts, his tone becomes serious and even severe. This feature is to be explained, perhaps, by the author's years of active participation in the State Legislature of Veracruz and in ministries of the federal government. Manuel Gutiérrez Nájera's "Historia de un peso bueno" (1892) has no very serious intention. The subject of this journalistic but graceful and amusing conversation with a coin is stated in the subtitle: "Economía humorística aplicada a la cuestión de la plata." Using this device, Gutiérrez Nájera laments the unwarranted low level of Mexico's international credit. We know that arbitrary measures taken by Benito Juárez had in fact resulted in a decline in European and American confidence in Mexico's financial integrity. When Porfirio Díaz eventually succeeded in balancing the national budget, at about the time when Gutiérrez Nájera was writing, the Mexican peso became one of the soundest currencies in the world.

Gutiérrez Nájera had once recounted the "Memorias de un paraguas" (1883), and several authors were later to tell the life stories of articles of clothing. The conception of "Aventuras de una casaca" (1890) by Guillermo Vigil y Robles was much more effectively realized by Francisco Rojas González in his first published story, "Historia de un frac" (1930).[6] The tragic autobiography of an aristocratic English frock-coat or *frac* proves an excellent, if not original, vehicle for the author's satire. Purchased from the elegant tailor shop of its birth in Regent Square by a ridiculous, newly-rich member of the Mexican government, the *frac* is taken to Mexico, where it describes with irony and indignation the absurd affectations of the ruling middle class.

One would have expected this line of stories to end abruptly after Carlos Villamil Castillo's mocking lampoon "Memorias de una lata de sardinas" (1949). Nevertheless, José Alvarado soon published *Memorias de un espejo* (1953), an admirable novelette without technical originality, but with a vision that is fresh and personal. An old abandoned mirror recalls with nostalgia scenes of daily life, moments of joy and disillusion that it witnessed over a period of generations. Alvarado himself has declared that *Memorias de un espejo* is "un relato muy malo,"[7] but such a judgment is far too harsh and probably derives from the author's new ideological position. In fact, this delicate monologue is expressed in prose colored with humor and irony; it sustains the reader's interest and reveals keen and subtle perception of human sentiment.

For Amado Nervo the irreconcilability of empirical science and idealistic philosophy was an enduring concern. He staged an effective debate, "Dos rivales" (1898?), between the opposing positions by personifying a cannon and a telescope. Bored with protecting the harbor entrance and the fortress, the cannon provokes a quarrel with the searching telescope. It argues in praise of action and against useless daydreaming. The history of the world, it says, is the record of triumphant cannon. But the telescope is quick to reply, "mientras tú cierras la entrada del puerto, yo abro la entrada del infinito."[8] The telescope credits itself for man's present state of knowledge about the earth and the universe, and it declares that the only hope for humanity rests in looking to the stars instead of killing one another in the mud. The futility of the discussion is indicated when the telescope, satisfied with its eloquence, notices that the cannon has fallen asleep.

Personifications of abstract qualities and ideas are abundant in didactic Mexican fiction. The soul has physical substance in Amado Nervo's "Los esquifes" (1921) and "El castillo de lo inconsciente" (1921), and again in Carlos Villamil Castillo's "¡Frank se ha vuelto loco!" (1949) and "El hombre que llevaba su alma a cuestas" (1949). Other examples include destiny, virtue, revenge, pain, and sorrow.[9] Death, the abstraction most constantly personified in Western literature since medieval times, has appeared with great frequency.

La vida portentosa de la Muerte, written in Zacatecas by the Franciscan friar Joaquín Bolaños and published in Mexico City in 1792, can be considered Mexico's first attempt at the novel form. One recognizes Bolaños as a forerunner of Fernández de Lizardi, especially in one chapter where Death mourns the passing of an ally, a favorite doctor. The biographical promise of the title is misleading; the work is merely a series of twelve disconnected episodes in each of which the figure of Death is present. Although the structure would seem to be typically picaresque, there really is no single central character to unite the episodes because, in each case, Death is portrayed in a different guise. *La portentosa vida de la Muerte* is interesting as a literary curiosity; as a novel, however, it is tedious, stilted and lacks integration.

Another churchman who employed allegory unimaginatively as a pretext for moralization was José Mariano Acosta Enríquez, a priest and poet from Querétaro. His novel *Sueño de sueños* (ca. 1800) closely resembles two earlier works: *Los sueños* (1627) by Francisco de Quevedo and *Sueños morales* (1727-1751) by Diego de Torres y Villarroel. Acosta Enríquez has his two models, Quevedo and Torres y Villarroel, both appear as characters in dialogue together with Cervantes. During the course of a pageant of moral symbols, Death and popular sayings in personified form, they discuss various aspects of eighteenth-century life.

The human desire to prolong life is reflected in tales of men bargaining with Death or of supernatural forces invoked through witchcraft. This wistful delusion is manifest too in the naive hypothesis that, if Death were to take on human form, she might herself become mortal. But in Mexico the supposed death of Death evokes no ingenuous optimism. "La defunción de la muerte" (1898), by Francisco Zárate Ruiz, is an apocalyptic vision in which Death, having fulfilled her destiny, is allowed to die but carries the rest of humanity along with her. In a more recent story, "La muerte ahorcada" (1963) by Héctor Gally, an Indian named Pedro Riquelme is traveling alone one night under a full moon when he comes upon a skeleton hanging from a tree. A scythe found beside the skeleton indicates to him that it is Death who for some mysterious reason has committed suicide. And in fact for six days after the skeleton is burned by the priest from Pedro's village no person dies in the whole republic. But on the seventh day Pedro disappears—with his scythe—, and on the eighth day his mother dies. Later some people claim they saw a human skeleton that same night carrying a scythe that glittered in the moonlight. Gally succeeds in creating here the folkloric quality essential to the so-called literary legend.

Gregorio López y Fuentes, by way of contrast, found the inspiration for his *Cuentos campesinos* (1940) in actual popular traditions, which he turned into literature. As personified by López y Fuentes in the parable "La inconformidad," Death illustrates the simple moral that illusions are necessary for happiness. Eternal life would be intolerable and knowledge of the future would bring only anxiety.

The figure of Death is introduced sometimes just to chill and terrify the reader (e.g., "En la orla del misterio," 1918, by Genaro Fernández MacGregor), but more often the aim is simple diversion. Death appears in Fernando Benítez's "Un extraño personaje" (1945) as a strange pallid little man wearing dark glasses and a brown overcoat, who repeatedly saves the narrator from untimely death. Lourdes Garza Quesada depicts Death as a beautiful girl ("Amigas siempre," 1961) in order to explain why so many young men are seduced by her, whereas for Elena Garro ("¿Qué hora es . . .?," 1964), Death is a sporty young man with a tennis racket.

Abstractions are conveniently represented by symbols, but, if there is to be drama and human interest, fictional characters must be convincing. Lorenzo Turrent Rozas thus portrays the pangs of conscience suffered by the narrator of "Cuento de febrero" (1940) through the materialization of a loquacious and quarrelsome alter ego or double. A nightmare was the source of "Diálogo de mi ingenio y mi consciencia" (1921), in which Alfonso Reyes watches two elements of his soul in personified form. The two versions of himself—one thin, the other dull and fat—are in a verbal struggle for control over his person, and he is helpless to intervene. The dreamer's anxiety increases when he realizes that the thin self (wit) is male and is courting the female conscience. Despite his protests that neither really knows anything about the other, they begin to reproduce themselves in a multitude of gnomes. As the dream fades, Reyes can hear his wit wooing conscience with passages quoted from the "Song of Solomon" and conscience replying with other passages. The fact that her quotations are actually apocryphal suggests that deception is the aim of both. The atmosphere of nightmare is recreated perfectly by Reyes at the same time that he tells a story that is more than allegory.

Unfortunately, few writers are as skilled as Alfonso Reyes in the creation of the symbolic story. Manuel Gutiérrez Nájera and Mariano Silva y Aceves are not at all convincing in their ponderous dialogues between Reason and Desire and Duty and Desire in "Dos y uno" (1877) and "El deseo de Juan Palomo" (1916), respectively. And Eduardo Lizalde's narrative of mind versus body, "Las cadenas" (1955), quickly degenerates into a tedious essay.

Guadalupe Dueñas is more engaging in "Mi chimpancé" (1954), where the theme of carnal desire and spiritual longing is expressed symbolically—the former by a chimpanzee in a cage, the latter by the narrator herself. The chimpanzee is tired of sitting in his cage getting no exercise and is determined to leave; the narrator, no longer so amused by his antics and vigor, agrees, for she knows that she will be happier once the matter is settled. The animal symbol in this story of personal frustration, written by Dueñas at the age of thirty-four, recalls the name Brother Ass with which St. Francis of Assisi referred to his body and its appetites.

Writers often amuse themselves by reworking familiar stories and motifs from classical or popular tradition. Fancifully they vary and combine elements from the store of Western literature in order to demonstrate their mastery of the literary medium or else to fit some personal message with a barb of irony. Julio Torri is such an artist with words, a cultured humorist in whose stories there is always an undercurrent of skepticism. In "El héroe" (1940), he tells of a hapless knight who cannot convince the people that he killed the dragon in a cowardly way and so should not be honored. Despite his protests he is swept along by publicity and fame and is obliged to wed the old and ugly princess. "Los unicornios" (1940) is Torri's tribute to the noble unicorn, which chose to perish in the Flood rather than submit to the terrible promiscuity of Noah's ark. The griffin too, says Torri, and certain kinds of dragons whose existence we know about from Chinese ceramics made the same commendable choice.

Another fabulous creature represented in Mexican fiction is the mermaid, a being allied to the siren of classical mythology. Two accounts of mermaids in the Gulf of Mexico are outstanding: "La sirena" (1868) by Justo Sierra, and "El hijo del mar" (1962) by Esteban Durán Rosado. Justo Sierra's eerie tale concerns a young man who is spellbound by the magical lay sung by an ugly hag known as Tía Ventura. In the eyes of the youth the old witch is a beautiful girl, but their union is an affront to nature and, as they embrace, a bolt of lightning strikes them to the bottom of the sea. When the immortal Tía Ventura emerges the lower half of her body has become that of a fish. Justo Sierra, who was born in the Gulf port of Campeche and spent his childhood in Mérida, Yucatán, composed this tale—one of his first *Cuentos románticos*—in the style of Gustavo Adolfo Bécquer while still a student at San Ildefonso. Esteban Durán Rosado also was educated in Mérida, and his writings reflect an intimate association with the Gulf Coast and the sea. The title-character of "El hijo del mar" is found as an infant in a basket on the Caribbean shore of Yucatán, perhaps abandoned by unknown parents, perhaps born of the sea. He grows up a strange, solitary lad who lives only for swimming with the fishes and the sea birds. Occasionally he hears the celestial voice of a mermaid, and one day he catches sight of her. From that time on he is obsessed, and he pursues her down deep into the sea to his death. In this story, Durán Rosado has created a stylistically perfect blend of artistic and popular elements. His forceful rhythmic prose, with constant reiteration of certain phrases, seems to lend the tale a sense of inevitability, of destiny, and to remove the events described into the realm of myth.

The highly conventionalized form of the fable has sometimes been adopted almost without modification by Vicente Riva Palacio (e.g., "El divorcio," 1896) and Gregorio López y Fuentes (e.g., "El hombre que miraba en la obscuridad," 1940). The latter's fable "Un pacto" (1940) can be interpreted as an allegorical satire of international politics. It tells of a pact among the carnivorous animals not to eat each other. Unfortunately, the insignificant ant refuses to agree and is eaten by the anteater, who in turn is eaten by the lynx, and so on until only the lion is left. Notable among other political parodies with animal protagonists are Carlos Toro's "Cuento del futuro" (1947) and "La asamblea de los animales" (1953) by Alfonso Reyes. The class struggle of the starving poor against the comfortable rich is represented in "La venganza de los perros" (1949), a more serious social allegory by Carlos Villamil Castillo, where a dog is forced by hunger to repudiate his class. He accepts an aristocratic St. Bernard's proposal that he serve the rich by preaching among his fellows the duty of accepting their situation. There is no doubt about the moral principle in this modern fable for when the "perro-Judas" emerges from the mansion carrying an old bone (his first payment), the other dogs set upon him and tear him to pieces. Such a story is obviously not a gratuitous trifle or a lyrical diversion from reality; nevertheless, its earnestness may be attributed in part to the form adopted—the apologue or moral tale which requires that a useful lesson be taught—and in the end it is above all a literary exercise.

On the other hand, some writers are content to limit their concern to the formal problems of a self-contained literary world. José Juan Tablada, for instance, had a very personal aim in writing his "Exempli gratia o fábula de los siete trovadores y de la *Revista moderna*" (1898) for publication in the first issue of that magazine as a challenge to the public. The troubadour's offer of song is rejected by the inhabitants of the castle, who prefer material pleasures—a lament for the artist in a philistine society which recalls Darío's short story, "El rey burgués" (1887). Simple amusement is the goal of *Fábulas sin moraleja y finales de cuentos* (1942), in which Francisco Monterde retells well-known fables by Aesop, La Fontaine and Iriarte, but with the conclusions altered in such a way that the original moral meanings are entirely lost. The fairy tales by Perrault, Andersen, Grimm and others he treats in a similar vein, considering how each one might have continued. The collection is full of lively humor arising from the incongruity of prosaic, realistic stories cast in the familiar fairy-tale mold.

Alfonso Reyes carried out two such literary exercises during 1913 in Madrid. One of them, "El fraile converso: diálogo mudo" (1920), is a continuation beyond the final curtain of a play (easily identified as *Measure for Measure*) by Shakespeare. Fray Pedro has been left to look after the drunken murderer Bernardino, but he does not know what to do with him without the guidance of his author. Fray Pedro is not used to having free will and complains to Shakespeare for abandoning him. He drags Bernardino aimlessly through the city streets until finally, despairing of any solution, he strangles him to be rid of the problem.[10] The other literary exercise alluded to above is his "Diálogo de Aquiles y Helena" (1920), a burlesque of the version that figures among the *Imaginary Conversations* (1824–1853) by the English classicist Landor. Reyes begins with an ironic description of the setting: "Escenario no muy vasto, no tan vasto como se asegura: la cabeza de Walter Savage Landor. Ambiente romano convencional."[11] He then picks up the conversation from where Landor had left it, but Reyes depicts Helen as a coquette and makes Aquiles confess that the vulnerability of his heel is really a case of gout inherited from his dissolute father. In another story, "Las babuchas" (1955), written in Madrid in 1915, Reyes displays his virtuosity magnificently. This fantastic narrative about a pair of magical slippers is a perfect imitation of the Arabian tales with their rich and extravagant imagery.

Of course, the adoption of a model from classical literature or mythology does not in itself guarantee success. Two noteworthy Mexican authors, Agustín Yáñez and José Emilio Pacheco, began their literary careers with unfortunate experiments in this vein. Yáñez attempts in the short novel *Isolda* (1943) to transplant the Arthurian legend of Tristam and Isoud the Fair to Mexico. The original story is followed closely, as Yáñez sends the young narrator to the lowland jungle to seek the hand of the beautiful Isolda la Blonda on behalf of his wealthy uncle Marcos. On the return journey they drink of an enchanted spring and fall in love, but their brief affair necessarily ends in tragedy. By weaving elements of witchcraft and popular Mexican mythology into the essentially European fabric, Yáñez gains an effect similar to the magical realism of Miguel Ángel Asturias. But the novel is not satisfactorily accommodated within the imposed framework. Moreover, since the characters fail to come to life, the reader is not caught up in their problems. Pacheco's "La sangre de Medusa" (1958), a more clumsy experiment than *Isolda,* simultaneously relates two parallel stories: in ancient Greece, the Perseus,

Medusa and Andromeda myth; and in Mexico, the story of Fermín Morales, a young man who is driven to murder his gorgon-like wife. Pacheco's carefully elaborated style is already apparent in this story, but his narrative technique is stiff and mechanical, still an inept imitation of Jorge Luis Borges.

Comic satire is one form of literary amusement that is frequently cultivated by accomplished writers wishing to demonstrate their wit and mastery of their craft and at the same time to ridicule certain social or artistic eccentricities. Any kind of human frailty provides a target for the satirist. The pedantry that is sometimes displayed by scholars has been a favorite subject for derision in literature ever since Aristophanes' comedy *The Clouds* (423 B.C.). A writer of vast erudition himself, Alfonso Reyes burlesques the German ideal of scholarship in a brilliantly humorous story, "En las repúblicas del Soconusco: memorias de un súbdito alemán" (1920). The form adopted is that of a learned treatise presented by a German resident of Tonalá to demonstrate how Mexico's economy rests on the toothpick industry. By expressing such an absurd subject in a lofty style, Reyes has achieved comic effects that are still fresh after nearly sixty years. "Sansón y Dalila" (1951) is a similar, though less subtle, parody by Rafael Solana. It consists of an address delivered to the French Academy by a famous archaeologist, Juan Hendrik Vandenpeerebum, who has just returned from a field trip to the Holy Land. Illustrating his lecture with slides of two quite ordinary clay-brick walls, Solana's extravagant scholar alleges that the walls themselves are really historical documents whose meaning he alone has been able to decipher after prolonged study of the arrangement of the bricks. They constitute, he states, a lengthy letter from Delilah and a short note in reply by Samson. With this ironic sketch, presumably, Solana is appealing for restraint by those archaeologists who, having discovered a few artifacts, offer fanciful reconstructions of whole periods of Mexico's pre-Hispanic cultures.

Salvador Elizondo's early stories were deliberate travesties of the forms and styles of consecrated authors. While these classic exercises in rhetorical discipline did serve to perfect his technical and stylistic versatility, they also constituted a challenge by the young writer, an assertion that the most respected authors' styles merely depended on particular effects that anyone could reproduce. Perhaps his most impressive exercise in mimicry is "Sila" (1962), which recreates with absolute fidelity the hermetic timeless world of "Luvina" (1953) and *Pedro Páramo* (1955) by Juan Rulfo. Together with his friend Leoncio, Paulino makes the long, arduous journey to Sila "para encontrar mis pasos muertos, para volver a la tierra de donde vine."[12] Sila is now an abandoned village inhabited only by a few dogs and by disembodied voices that are still to be heard in the empty streets speaking of violence, cruelty, incest, and love. The villagers were brutally murdered during the Cristero rebellion and their souls are not at rest. Under the influence of the voices, Paulino becomes delirious and kills Leoncio with a machete, thus contributing more blood to the tragic history of Sila. The voice of Paulino's mother speaks to him: "— Paulino, hijo, es demasiado tarde. Tu recuerdo se ha perdido en el camino de Ajol. No eres más que una sombra llena de sangre. Nada te pertenece . . . ni tu muerte."[13] Elizondo is cosmopolitan in outlook, he is well-read in English, German, Italian, and French literatures, and his work generally reveals a preoccupation with all forms of artistic expression. Motion pictures are of particular interest to Elizondo, who has both made experimental films and written film criticism. "Narda o el verano" (1966), whose title suggests a parody of the short stories written by Agustín Yáñez, is really a pastiche of assembled *clichés* from the French and Italian "new wave" films of the early 1960s: the lazy Italian summer by the sea, a Swiss girl, a German, an African Negro, witchcraft, eroticism, murder. Ironically, this film parody has itself been made into a movie with Acapulco as the setting.[14]

The rhetorical imitation of a great model does not always seek to parody or devalue the original, but may be intended to emulate and reaffirm the values of that original. Such was the case of *El Dr. Fu Chang Li* (1945), written by Octavio G. Barreda as a vehicle for stating his position in a literary polemic. Barreda insists that the story is true, and he uses the names of real people, dates, and even provides footnotes. The story relates how the author and Antonio Sánchez Barbudo go to a Chinese restaurant one night after finishing work at the newspaper *Excélsior* on Bucareli Street. They are astonished when the proprietor introduces himself as a former professor and engages them in a discussion of Spanish and Mexican literature. In his luxurious apartments behind the squalid restaurant kitchen they put on kimonos and skull-caps and drink tea; later, they are joined by María Asúnsolo, an Argentine named Señor Bo, and a certain Ingeniero Gavaldón. Before long, Gavaldón, who is drunk and offensive, has provoked a riot. María is hysterical and there is blood all over the rug. Just as the police are arriving Barreda and Sánchez Barbudo escape into the street still wearing kimonos and skull-caps. Days later Barreda meets María at an exhibition and refers to the incident but she doesn't know what he is talking about. The Chinese restaurant proprietor swears that there are no living quarters behind the kitchen and that he knows nothing of the man, the affair or, indeed of literature.

The period of the Second World War brought intense dis-illusionment with idealistic values in Mexico. As a result, literature dealing primarily with personal or aesthetic problems was severely attacked, and to most critics only the social realities of the Revolution or the national heritage were acceptable subjects for art. As director of two important literary magazines of the period, *Letras de México* and *El hijo pródigo*, Octavio G. Barreda was at the centre of the con-troversy. In the story just outlined, and particularly in the person of Dr. Fu Chang Li, Barreda seems to have expressed his support for the cosmopolitan cause. The key to this interpretation lies in Barreda's description of Fu Chang Li's speech:

> Hablaba y construía bien el español y a no ser por las erres que se le licuaban en eles fácilmente se le hubiera tomado por un mexicano. Forzando el parecido, pudiera haberse dicho de él que era una mezcla de Bojórquez, de Marte R. Gómez y de Genaro Estrada.[15]

Estrada was a diplomat, historian, bibliographer and colonialist writer; Juan de Díos Bojórquez was an agronomical engineer and businessman, a diplomat and a newspaper columnist who published more than a dozen books on the Revolution; whereas Marte R. Gómez was the Secretary of Agriculture at the time. All three men had expressed views of literature similar to those which Barreda ridicules by putting them in the mouth of the absurd Dr. Fu Chang Li, e.g.,

> Ling Tang, mi maestlo, ahola gozando de los lotos celestiales, nos decía que los españoles, y peldóneme usted señol Baleda que haga extensivo el ejemplo a los mexicanos, elan como los latones—mis-teliosos pelo tontos; soble todo, cuando se mueven fuela de su ambi-ente. Ahí tiene usted el caso del plopio Juan Lamón. . . . Y este síntoma también se lefleja en la litelatula de los países de ustedes. El doctol González Maltínez, pol ejemplo, hablando del cielzo, de la nieve que cuble los campos . . . nieve que jamás he visto aquí. . . . Alfonso Leyes, quemando la almendla de sus ojos, en panegílicos y tlatados de los gliegos. . . . Jaime Toles . . .
> —¿Qué Toles?—inquirió Antonio.
> —Toles Bodet,—contestó el chino.[16]

Barreda makes his position clear by adopting as his model a story by Spanish America's foremost champion of cosmopolitanism, Jorge Luis Borges. The tribute is implicit not only in the nature of the theme and the discursive prose style, but in such typically Borgean passages as the following:

> La infinidad de mundos, la multiplicidad en círculos concéntricos, hasta el infinito, de vidas o planos de existencia, cada una de ellas plena

> y propia, sin más relaciones con las otras que el leve roce de un transitorio contacto, o de su coexistencia. En ese aturdimiento, nos era difícil interpretar al supuesto Dr. Fu Chang Li.[17]

Besides this, Dr. Fu Chang Li—born in Canton, educated at Oxford, Columbia and Leipzig, professor of Spanish literature at Shanghai University—bears more than a coincidental resemblance to Borges' Dr. Yu Tsun, former professor of English at the Hochschule of Tsingtao and, later, secret agent for Germany in Staffordshire. Significantly, the story by Borges in which Dr. Yu Tsun appears—"El jardín de senderos que se bifurcan" (1941)—is an attempt to show that all literature is necessarily a linear falsification of reality, which by nature is chaotic.

Convinced of the impossibility of transcribing reality, Borges and his followers have sought to purify literature of its sentimental, personal element. They prefer not to consider life, which is amorphous and bewildering, but to pursue the formal beauty of intricate puzzles and designs. For Borges himself though, the choice is not merely frivolous social irresponsibility:

> En . . . todos mis cuentos, hay una parte intelectual y otra—más importante, según creo—, el sentimiento de la soledad, de la angustia, de la inutilidad, del carácter misterioso del universo, del tiempo, y lo que es más importante: de nosotros mismos, para decirlo de una vez: de mí mismo.[18]

This underlying view of man in a chaotic universe is what gives to the works of Borges the human validity that is lacking in so many of his imitators.

It has been remarked that nothing is explicable but that which man himself creates. "A circle is not absurd," says Sartre. "It is adequately accounted for by the rotation of a segment of a straight line around one of its extremities. But then there is no such thing as a circle."[19] It is purely intellectual conception. Aesthetic creativity seeks to widen experience, to improve on nature as nearly everything in music is an improvement on nature. Art becomes a game of infinite possibilities, a playful structure of the universe founded on the author's essential skepticism.

Mexican literature has its most worthy disciple of Borges in Salvador Elizondo, notably in such stories as "El ángel azul" (1967) and "La historia según Pao Cheng" (1966). Although "El ángel azul" lacks Borges's clarity, it is a marvel of artistic precision and erudition. The theme—the cold vanity of woman—serves only as a focus in an elaborately complex structure. A story abstracted from the Faust legend and the film named in the title emerges from a labyrinth of occult symbols and allusions both literary and cinematic.[20] More obviously Borgean is the metaphysical fantasy "La historia según Pao Cheng," an ingenious variation on an oriental concept of fictitious existence. Sitting by a stream one day 3500 years ago, Pao Cheng imagined how future history might be. He saw himself in a strange city in front of a certain house. Through the window he could see a man writing something called "La historia según Pao Cheng." Suddenly, he understood that he himself was only a memory of this man and that if the man were to forget him he would cease to exist. The writer had just written the words "si ese hombre me olvida moriré" when he realized that he would have to go on forever writing the story of Pao Cheng, because, if his character were forgotten and died, then he too would disappear for he was only a thought in the mind of Pao Cheng.[21]

The pure abstraction of a mathematical system is embodied in "Poseidonis" (1956) by the architect, painter, poet, and mathematician Mauricio Gómez Mayorga. Poseidon was one of several islands thought by some to be part of Atlantis, the mythic continent that, according to Plato, disappeared into the ocean 12,500 years ago. In Gómez Mayorga's story, absolute symmetry and geometric perfection serve to purify the souls of the inhabitants of Poseidonis. The island is situated exactly in the middle of the Atlantic; it is absolutely flat and has sheer cliffs rising 100 meters above the sea; in shape it is a perfect circle having a diameter of precisely 1000 kilometers and thus a circumference of 3141 kilometers, 592 meters, 653 milimeters . . ., constituting a religious tribute to the interminable Sacred Number: 3.14159263. . . . Precisely in the center of the island is the city Plutón of exactly 10,000,000 inhabitants, and at its center is a cylindrical palace 100 meters in diameter. When it is revealed to the king in a dream that he is the island's 1000th successive ruler, he knows that he must go to the circular table and there press the button that will lower the island continent into the ocean, drowning all the inhabitants. They will return to disorder and at last be free of their symmetrical history and their sterile, joyless existence. In this story Gómez Mayorga has epitomized the conception of art as a purely aesthetic object which provides the same cerebral pleasure as that derived from following the solution of a complicated puzzle or game of chess. Aesthetic harmony and beauty depend here on strictly geometrical, empty form. But the author was actually inspired only in part by his interest in pure form and the fascinating Atlantis legend. "Poseidonis" expresses in classic utopian terms a very modern preoccupation—the apocalyptic vision of the world being destroyed by merely pressing a button, a theme that provides a constant stimulus to those authors who work within the form known as science fiction.

The cerebral compositions of Jorge Luis Borges have not found fertile soil in Mexico. They first became known there during the 1940s, directly from available texts, through enthusiastic reviews,[22] and in polemical writings like *El Dr. Fu Chang Li* by Octavio G. Barreda. It was only during the 1950s and 1960s that a few young Mexican writers began to emulate his intellectual and geometric puzzles, and then only as a stage in their development of a personal style.[23] Although Borges is still greatly admired for his ingenuity and the formal beauty and clear, direct language of his work, it has been generally recognized that his structured world is not capable of being transferred or repeated.

◇◇◇◇◇◇◇

The playful fantasies treated in this chapter were created, for the most part, for mere amusement or pastime. We admire the elegance, imagination, and enormous versatility of Alfonso Reyes in his cleverly humorous stories or his witty variations of classical literature and Shakespeare; of special interest in the short pieces by Julio Torri are his delightful irony and the fine precision of his prose; and Amado Nervo's essay-like narratives feature a curious use of lyricism in a context of logical disputation, the result of an excursion by the poet into the fascinating world of science. One does not read Gutiérrez Nájera's accounts of the adventures of an umbrella, a coin, or a comet in order to be instructed, but simply for their delicacy and grace. Stories which have inanimate objects as protagonists are not intended to reveal hidden aspects of life, but simply to provide the novelty of a fresh point of view. For the authors as well as for the reader, these are ingenuous, escapist entertainments in which reality is freely transformed for the purpose of sustaining the sense of wonder that is essential to the human spirit.

---CHAPTER IV---

Utopian and Science Fiction

Many philosophers and writers have entertained the idea of a possible state of human perfection towards which civilization could develop. The best known and most influential work describing such an ideal commonwealth is Plato's *Republic*, but this branch of literature has come to be designated as "utopian," after the romance *Utopia* (Gr. *ou*, "not," *topos*, "a place") published in 1516 by the English Renaissance humanist Sir Thomas More. It may be, however, that More intended a play with the word *eutopia* (Gr. *eu*, "good," *topos* "place"), as is suggested by the portrait of communal equality and wise government in his imaginary island. Most of the subsequent utopian novels fit into one or the other of these two categories: either dream projections of exotic adventures in an ideal state impossible of attainment (e.g., Tomasso Campanella's *Civitas solis*, 1623; Francis Bacon's *New Atlantis*, 1627), or more practical, highly persuasive outlines for a better society than any presently in existence (e.g., Edward Bellamy's *Looking Backward*, 1888; H. G. Wells' *A Modern Utopia*, 1905). An extensive criticism of society may be implied in the latter type by the sharp contrast between the real world and the fanciful creation.

One form of utopian fiction, the pastoral romance, was very fashionable in Italy and Spain at the end of the sixteenth and the beginning of the seventeenth centuries. The conventionalized pastoral was an extremely artificial presentation of rustic life, with idealized shepherds discoursing in inflated language on the subject of love. Bernardo de Balbuena's precious romance, *El siglo de oro en las selvas de Erífile* (1608), follows very closely the prototype of the genre, the *Arcadia* (1504), by the Neapolitan Sannazaro. On the other hand, in *Los sirgueros de la Virgen sin original pecado* (1620), Francisco Bramón makes use of the genre then in fashion to explain the doctrine of the Immaculate Conception. Instead of the usual rhapsodies of love addressed to the shepherdesses, the priest Bramón sings praises only of the Virgin. Welcome relief comes when the characters arrange a celebration in honor of the Doctrine, a celebration that includes a lively *auto* for the instruction of the Indians.

A modern Mexican version of the pastoral romance, *En el nuevo Aztlán* (1949), is an ingenuous novel of escapism and adventure written by María de Lourdes Hernández. Here the shepherds are replaced by idealized Indians in an idyllic setting that is obviously indebted to James Hilton's *Lost Horizon* (1933). Hidden from civilization in this Aztec Shangri-La, the descendants of Moctezuma and Cuauhtémoc have reconstructed the great city of Tenochtitlán.

The description of fantastic utopias is a favorite vehicle of the satirist; he objectifies his theories of the perfect society in order to condemn by implication the corresponding features of his own. The modern utopian is seldom extravagantly idealistic, however, and the reforms he envisions are less comprehensive than those recommended in earlier programs of reconstruction. Occasionally, he will be content to address himself to a single objectionable characteristic, which he exaggerates in his allegory for the purpose of censure. Such is the underlying motive of several of the texts of one eminent representative of the group known as the Ateneo de la Juventud, Julio Torri. His "Era un país pobre" (1917) is a disdainful portrait of a once-prosperous country where the fluctuating value of literature is recorded on the stock exchange. Formerly, while the quality of literature had been high, the economy had remained sound and there was general prosperity. Written in 1917, Julio Torri's message for Mexican authors at that time of national upheaval is clear when a disastrous collapse of the stock market in his fictitious country is attributed to the public's having become pessimistic and turning away from literature. Up to this time, literature has been a miraculous source of spiritual purification, but now it serves only to express tortured ideas and complicated inventions. This amusing association of literary value with the stock market was repeated twenty years later by Antonio Castro Leal for an elaborate but uninspired story entitled "La literatura no se cotiza" (1937), in which he sought to ridicule the United States rather than to extol the value of art.

The fine elegance of Julio Torri's style and his preference for exotic subjects caused him to be regarded as an aesthete who was unconcerned about the social realities of Mexico. Yet Torri does speak to the particular problems of his nation but in such an oblique way that the criticism does not stand out. How well he integrates his comment into the work of art can be illustrated by reference to "La conquista de la luna" (1917), a story depicting the social consequences of the invasion of the moon. The moon people offer no resistance to the invaders from earth and the conquest is easily accomplished. The only form of opposition to the adventure has been the usual ineffectual café debates. Inevitably, occupation leads to the adoption of alien fashions not only in clothes but even in social customs. From many pointed references it is clear that this concise relation is above all a satire of the excesses of the symbolist poets, such as Leopoldo Lugones (e.g., *Lunario sentimental,* 1909), who let themselves be directed from abroad. But also implicit here is a warning of a threat to Mexican culture, one constituted by the huge financial investment from the United States. Even if the foreign influence expresses itself first and most obviously in commerce and industry, it will soon become all-pervasive.

The United States has very few champions among the writers of Latin America; this is especially true in the case of Mexico. A notable exception is Diego Cañedo [Guillermo Zárraga] who, although perhaps better known for his light entertaining fantasies, has written ambitious works of social importance. During the Second World War, Cañedo was dismayed by the general acceptance in Mexico of Nazi propaganda. In order to influence public opinion against Hitler and in support of the United States, he wrote an impressive futuristic novel which he entitled *El réferi cuenta nueve* (1943). This optimistic work, which purports to be the published version of a manuscript mysteriously written in 1961 but discovered in 1938, records the Nazi invasion of America by way of Panama and Central America. The protagonist Rodrigo Guerrero typifies the popular admiration for Hitler in such statements as

> —Sin embargo—argumentó Rodrigo—no cabe duda que ese hombre está transformando Alemania. Por el trabajo, el orden y la disciplina está haciendo milagros. Lo que aquí en México necesitamos es un Hitler.[1]

The tyrannical behavior of the Nazis occupying Mexico while they prepare to strike at the United States, convinces Rodrigo, finally, that the most important quality of life is liberty. He then urges his fellow Mexicans to forget their traditional resentment of the United States:

"Tendremos que estar con los Estados Unidos si se trata de defender esa libertad y el sentido cristiano de la vida, y la dignidad del espíritu humano."[2]

Cañedo continues to play with time in his next novel *Palamás, Echevete y yo o el lago asfaltado* (1945) where, like Voltaire and Lizardi, he employs an observer from another civilization to make objective judgments on contemporary society. There is the difference, however, that Cañedo's outsider is a time-traveler, a professor from some future university, who stops over on an excursion he is making through time with an apparatus much like the one described by H. G. Wells in *The Time Machine* (1895). When the narrator and a friend accompany Professor Palamás back through time, they have many adventures including a narrow escape from the Holy Inquisition; they also gain insights into Mexican history. Palamás is critical of the current government and warns of increasing state oppression of the individual in the near future, but he assures his companions of the ultimate triumph of human understanding, dignity and tolerance. Implicit in the subtitle of the novel is the author's concept of time and history. The striking image of a lake covered with asphalt suggests that the changes brought by time are only superficial, that Tenochtitlán built on Lake Texcoco survives even today in Mexico's modern capital. In Cañedo's view, time has no reality; there is only good and evil existing in an eternal present.

Utopian thought is most often expressed today through literature of science fiction. In a world that is characterized by constant innovation, the socially constructive utopia will necessarily look towards the future. And the quality of that future will be determined largely by the tremendous advances being made in scientific technology and their effect on human life. The earliest Mexican work that could be regarded as science fiction was written in Mérida in 1773 by a Franciscan named Manuel Antonio de Rivas. The friar's untitled story describes a congress of historians and chroniclers resident on the moon. The lunar academy is meeting to hear an address concerning the state of science on earth by a certain Onésimo Dutalón, a French scientist who has arrived in a flying machine. Dutalón had constructed his strange machine in France but, fearing charges of witchcraft from the Inquisition, he took it to Libya for the test flights. Ironically, the author of the story was himself persecuted by the Inquisition in Mexico for his rash ideas.[3]

The ideal society towards which man presumably aspires would logically be comprised only of ideal people. Hence the subject of eugenics or genetic control arises of necessity. Yet it is one of the dilemmas of modern Utopia that—against logic, against reason—this subject invariably evokes a negative emotional response. As Professor J. C. Garrett has observed, "we want evolutionary advance, but we don't want the process to go too far. Utopians of the future must be recognizably related to us; we have no real enthusiasm for supermen or evolutionary non-human deities."[4]

Science fiction in Mexican literature, we have seen, dates from an untitled story written in 1773 by a Franciscan friar (Manuel Antonio de Rivas). But it was one hundred and forty-six years later when Mexico produced its first full-length novel of science fiction. The novel, *Eugenia* (Mérida, 1919), is a description of life in Villautopia, capital of the Subconfederation of Central America in the year 2218. The author, Eduardo Urzáis, envisions a complete city of the future where the state exercises absolute control over society. Everything is impersonal and perfectly administered; teaching, for instance, is conducted by means of hypnotism. Wars in the twentieth and twenty-first centuries brought universal disarmament and the abolition of national boundaries, thereby freeing the men from obligatory military service. Instead, the robust, physically attractive, and psychologically balanced males are selected to serve as Official Reproducers of the Species for one year, their sole duty being to beget twenty children. The government program for euthenasia and the selective sterilization of all physically or mentally defective persons and of everyone at the age of fifty has eliminated the need for prisons, insane asylums, and hospitals for the incurable and has released large sums of money for the eradication of poverty. But Urzáis—himself a doctor in a mental institution for fourteen years—does not welcome such an ideal state; gradually he makes his utopia assume the nightmare qualities of the dystopia that Aldous Huxley was to describe years later in his *Brave New World* (1932).

Jorge Useta [José Ugarte] warns that monsters may be created in "El joven Godofredo y sus glándulas" (1932), and Eglantina Ochoa Sandoval doubts whether man is prepared to accept objective evidence of what actually constitutes a superior being. She makes the point in "Breve reseña histórica" (1962), where a German scientist commits suicide when the marvelous baby he has created in his laboratory begins to manifest the features of the Negro race. And Antonio Sánchez Galindo, in "Orden de colonización" (1966), predicts a new revolution in the Soviet Union based on the issue of state genetic control.

Wisely conducted, scientific research can bring undoubted benefits to mankind but since man himself is by nature imperfect, human strife can be expected to persist. Francisco Urquizo's naive, Jules Verne-type novel, *Mi tío Juan* (1934), tells of a marvelous variety of wheat that the protagonist develops from Indian, Arabian, and Egyptian strains. The discovery could solve the problem of hunger throughout the world but, unfortunately, international business interests persuade their governments to obstruct its distribution. The protagonist outwits the authorities and succeeds in getting the secret formula to the people. The remainder of the novel is devoted to his superhuman but futile attempts to force universal peace upon the nations of the world.

The title of "Orestes" (1964) by Alfredo Leal Cortés recalls the legendary figure whose blood sacrifice was required by Nemesis and the Furies. The fatal error of arrogant pride is the theme of this new personal drama set in the distant future. Orestes, the most learned and famous of men, has grown vain since all life's mysteries have been revealed to him. His confidence is shattered one day when he glimpses something that his mind can hardly accept—a common ant. He is profoundly shocked for he knows that all insects were eliminated from the planet a century earlier. Their reappearance will have terrible consequences for mankind. Orestes is overcome with panic and, in accordance with the requirements of poetic justice, he is devoured by millions of ants. One of the aims of science fiction is precisely the instilling of a sense of humility into the reader. While man's actual and potential technological achievements are the substance of science fiction, they are always overshadowed by an insistence on human frailty.

Most of today's authors of science fiction (also known as "speculative fiction" or "fantastic realism") insist on a clear distinction between that mode of expression and literary fantasy. Futuristic stories qualify as science fiction only if they are plausible extrapolations of present conditions. Science fiction should deal only in possibilities; fantasy may freely abandon verisimilitude. Kingsley Amis expresses the distinction plainly but his open intolerance of fantasy leads him to oversimplification:

> While science fiction . . . maintains a respect for fact or presumptive fact, fantasy makes a point of flouting these; for the furniture of robots, spaceships, techniques, and equations it substitutes elves, broomsticks, occult powers, and incantations.[5]

The link with reality is emphasized by Amis in his working definition of science fiction:

> Science fiction is that class of prose narrative treating of a situation that could not arise in the world we know, but which is hypothesized on the basis of some innovation in science or technology, or pseudo-science or pseudo-technology, whether human or extra-terrestrial in origin.[6]

The well-known scientist and author Isaac Asimov defines the form more succinctly as "that branch of literature that is concerned with the impact of science and technological advance upon human beings."[7]

A new, powerful kind of magic, science has largely usurped the place of superstition in the modern world and can therefore be called upon to compensate for the imaginary world it destroyed. Any theme —religious, poetic, psychological, social or political—can be accommodated within the sphere of science fiction, although the results have not always been fortunate. A favorite among the many themes treated is the threat of atomic radiation and destruction; others include poverty, starvation, colonial exploitation, and over-population. Primarily a literature of thoughtful and instructive entertainment, science fiction has only partly recovered its good reputation, which was destroyed by the so-called B. E. M.'s (i.e., bug-eyed monsters) and the menace-to-earth theme that characterized American and British pulp magazine fantasy of the 1920s and 1930s. Mexican authors, having come late to science fiction, have generally avoided the same error.[8]

The conclusion of the Second World War with the atomic destruction of Hiroshima and Nagasaki marks a decided change in the suppositions made about possible inhabitants of other parts of the universe. As we have observed, speculation about the future is really disguised speculation about the present. Man's ability to create atomic weapons and his decision to use them seem to indicate that his sense of morality is inadequate to his surprising technological achievements. Before the war, aliens from other planets were drawn as horrible monsters eager to devour unwary humans; later the general view came to be that any living creatures in the universe will be superior to man, both technologically and morally. Naive and earnest prescriptions for an ideal society are offered as the teachings of missionaries from Venus or Mars (e.g., *El mundo que soñamos*, 1956, by Pedro Camarena; *Hablemos de Venus*, 1958, by Salvador Villanueva Medina). On the other hand, the superior aliens may be very reluctant to establish relations with earth men (e.g., "Contraorden," 1968, by Alfredo Cardona Peña).

The possibility of space exploration so fascinated the painter, writer and vulcanologist known as Dr. Atl that he returned time and again to the theme. It first appeared in his *Un hombre más allá del universo* (1935), which he described in the prologue as not a novel of adventures but "una abstrusa sinfonía de la suposición—el rumor de extraños sonidos en el frío silencio de la mente."[9] The work is at once an essay in which Dr. Atl develops his ideas on physics and astronomy and a narrative about a visitor who has come to earth from a distant region of the universe. The fantastic journey was made in a strange vehicle called the "Cristal Cósmico," a 32-faceted polyhedron of an unknown material and capable of enormous velocities. In the novel *El Padre Eterno, Satanás y Juanito García* (1938), already considered briefly in Chapter Two, Dr. Atl's Mexican scientist García discovers certain non-electrical elements from which he constructs a large crystal polyhedron capable of annihilating time and space and of transforming the world. Finally, the crystal polyhedron recurs in "El hombre que se quedó ciego en el espacio" (1941) as the power source for a rocket ship sighted from earth and reported as an unidentified flying object. The occupant of the ship is setting out to explore the limits of the universe. Although the scientific aspects of Dr. Atl's fiction are unconvincing, his impressions of travel through space are prophetic.

The most complete expression of the theme of space travel is found in a comic fantasy published in 1968 by a university student named Carlos Olvera. His novel, *Mejicanos en el espacio*, ostensibly speculation about Mexico in the year 2147, is in fact an allegorical satire of present-day life. The ironic tone is immediately apparent in the dedication: "Con todo mi respeto a Laika, la pionera" and even in the title, where the "j" of "mejicanos" indicates the future triumph of extreme conservatism in Mexican politics. But the author's many sharp criticisms of present government policies are diluted in the general humor of the work. *Mejicanos en el espacio* is neither entirely frivolous nor entirely serious; the general approach is fanciful, and yet most of the details are well-founded in contemporary reality. Obviously an example of the recent movement to replace literary Spanish with colloquial language, this slangy space fantasy of astronauts and Martians, "biocibernetics" and miscellaneous futuristic contrivances also manages to identify areas in need of social and political reform as Mexico moves suddenly into the twentieth century.

As an instrument of "social diagnosis and warning,"[10] science fiction interprets and judges society; it seeks to anticipate the stresses of a changing world and to show the way to emotional as well as physical survival. Now that science has developed beyond the comprehension of most educated people, it has taken on something of the aura of mystery and menace that primitive man sensed in every feature of the natural world. Thus in literature, the scientist is often cast, perhaps unfairly, as a living threat to civilization. In 1945, the year of Hiroshima, the editor of *Excélsior*, Manuel Becerra Acosta, published a collection of short stories called *Los domadores*. The title story is a parable in which the acknowledged winner of a circus competition for animal trainers is one who has dissuaded three illustrious scientists from continuing their research into more ingenious means of human destruction. He describes his achievement in these terms:

> Yo he domado animales más peligrosos que los tigres de Bengala; yo he educado animales más venenosos que la cobra; yo he hecho inofensivas a bestias más traidoras que el chacal, yo he convertido al más terrible, al más fiero, al más hipócrita de los animales. Yo soy domador de hombres.[11]

But we know that in reality there can be no such tamer of men, and when the judges look for him to award the prize he has vanished. The lesson then is that self-control is both possible and necessary but the control of others is an illusion.

Most important among the themes found in science fiction is a concern for the dangerous implications of utopian thought. The headlong pursuit of technological progress, though intellectually appealing, may bring terrible emotional strains. As early as 1909 the poet Amado Nervo considered in "Cien años de sueño" and again in "Los congelados" (1921) the psychological problems of suspended animation. Nervo anticipates the application of the process to long journeys through space, but even his fertile imagination is surpassed by that of today's Cryonic Society of New York, according to which suspended animation could be the key to immortality.[12] The tragic plight of an unadapted youth living in a future Orwellian civilization on the planet Ceres is described by María Elvira Bermúdez in "Vuelo en la noche" (1968), which she published under the pseudonym Raúl Weil.

The relative physical comforts enjoyed by Western society are due, principally, to the mechanization of industry. But the impact of machine technology extends into our daily life to an ever-increasing degree. Since we speak of "feeding" vast quantities of information into computers as if they were living organisms, the question of whether the machine is servant or master of man is an obvious theme for the writer of science fiction. Alfredo Cardona Peña has composed a number of stories on the subject of autonomous robots, e.g., "Un interesante reportaje" (1966) and "Testigo ocular" (1966); and in "La niña de Cambridge" (1966) what he terms "el primer drama auténtico de la cibernética" unfolds when men treat computers as if they were machines and as a result are charged with a new offence: "crueldad criminal con máquinas pensantes."[13]

While he was living in New York City in 1917, Martín Luis Guzmán was greatly impressed by contemporary technological achievements. Under this influence he wrote his only work of science fiction, an excellent story entitled "Cómo acabó la guerra en 1917," in which he conceives of an electronic brain capable of storing and analyzing an infinite amount of information. It is employed by the government for the censoring of all private and commercial correspondence. From this varied information, the machine draws cryptic conclusions that eventually begin to reveal a terrible message: the world, it seems, is about to destroy itself. As the final day looms near the feverish operator is driven to madness.

The apocalyptic theme is a constant of science fiction in Mexico just as in the United States, Britain, Germany, France, and Russia. Some authors foresee the world laid waste without a living thing remaining; others believe that the more primitive creatures might survive the holocaust. "Cinq-heures-sans-coeur" (1940) is a scathing satire of the cold materialism that Bernardo Ortiz de Montellano imagines he sees dominating the world. In his vision, the earth is inherited by tiny heartless creatures who understand and enjoy nothing during their brief life. The name describes their nature, and its ready translatability suggests that the problem is not limited to a single nation—"Cinq-heures-sans-coeur," otherwise "Cinco horas sin corazón." The last heirs to the earth are the horses in Amado Nervo's "La última guerra"(1898?); in Rafael Bernal's fantastic novel *Su nombre era muerte* (1947), it falls to the flies; to the apes in "Charles Darwin IV" (1964) by Jaime Cardeña; and in "Los blátidos"(1967) by Froylán Manjarrez, it reverts to the cockroaches. Final words for a dead planet are spoken by Guadalupe Dueñas in "Y se abrirá el Libro de la Vida" (1957), the style and images of which are closely based on Chapters 6, 7, and 8 of the Book of Revelation—all is darkness, water turns to stone, every living being crumbles into ashes, and the stars and the moon are extinguished:

> La dimensión de la sombra abarca la inmensidad.
>
> Y todo es destruido. Sólo la Voz del Señor flota sobre la nada.
>
> Y se abrirá el Libro de la Vida.[14]

◇◇◇◇◇◇◇

There is no established tradition of utopian and science fiction in Mexico. With the exception of Amado Nervo, Julio Torri, Dr. Atl, Bernardo Ortiz de Montellano, and Guadalupe Dueñas—whose stories are quite personal—the authors of most of the selections discussed in the present chapter have consciously subscribed to foreign literary conventions, even when inspired by local conditions. Bernardo de Balbuena and Francisco Bramón wrote typically European pastoral novels in America. Francisco Urquizo and Diego Cañedo reproduced in Mexico utopian fantasy in the style of H. G. Wells. Pedro Camarena and Salvador Villanueva Medina nationalized American pulp-magazine science fiction while others, more discerning, profited from the best stories of Ray Bradbury, Robert A. Heinlein, and Isaac Asimov. Carlos Olvera's novel *Mejicanos en el espacio* is important not for its futuristic vision, but as a contribution to the campaign now being waged by young writers in Spanish America to replace literary Spanish with colloquial speech. The most artistically polished of Mexican science fiction is that of Alfredo Cardona Peña, but even his work is not entirely original. Science fiction is a relatively new form in Mexican literature, although the *modernistas* were fascinated by the spiritual implications of science for man. It is true that more than half a century ago Martín Luis Guzmán published his story concerning a huge computer ("Cómo acabó la guerra in 1917"), but he wrote it in New York City. Several of the young writers of Mexico today are looking beyond the national boundaries and are finding an involvement in issues that preoccupy the modern world, e.g., the possibilty of widespread famine and poverty, the morality of genetic manipulation and the threat of atomic destruction. In many cases, their lack of originality of expression is compensated for by their enthusiasm and concern.

Utopian and science fiction writing in Mexico naturally reflects the limitations that are implicit in the form. It suffers, for instance, from obvious artistic deficiencies. The characters are not individuals but matchstick-men representative of their species. They are neglected consciously, however, in order to draw attention away from their psychology and direct it to the sociological or philosophical question that constitutes the theme. A frequent criticism of science fiction is that its appeal is purely cerebral, that it deals with novel ideas and ingenious extrapolations but rarely moves us to emotion. Indeed the romantic reader may dislike the quantifying, dispassionate approach to the universe and to human existence, but of all the varieties of fantasy, science fiction is the most closely linked to the problems of the real world. This is not a form of poetic or escapist amusement; on the contrary, it is a sincere expression of concern, a cry of warning that a present which is lacking in human virtues and wisdom must certainly lead to a disastrous future.

Part 2
Imagination

CHAPTER V

The Unconscious

Literary fantasy ranges so widely in spirit and purpose that it can be satisfactorily defined only in terms of its subject matter. C. S. Lewis, for example, conceives of it simply as "any narrative that deals with impossibles and preternaturals."[1] At any event, whether a fantasy is intended to horrify or to entertain, whether aestheticist or didactic, it is essentially an arbitrary recombination of elements already existing in reality. These are the "fixities" and "definites" of the celebrated distinction between fancy and imagination elaborated by Coleridge in Chapter XIII of *Biographia Literaria* (1817):

> The IMAGINATION . . . I consider . . . as a repetition in the finite mind of the eternal act of creation in the infinite I AM . . . .
>
> FANCY, on the contrary, has no other counters to play with but fixities and definites. The Fancy is indeed no other than a mode of Memory emancipated from the order of time and space; . . . But equally with the ordinary memory the Fancy must receive all its materials ready made from the law of association.[2]

Yet, although Coleridge's idea has had considerable influence in Romantic literary criticism, it would be well to note that it is really a distinction without a difference because not even the Imagination actually creates anything new. Imagination is no less an associative or combinatory process than is fancy (and its product fantasy). The true distinction between these two modes of literature lies rather in the author's attitude towards the real world. The author of fantasy generally is not interested in the real world except as a source of materials which he employs in a particular way and for a particular purpose. The author of works of imagination, on the other hand, is concerned with exploring the nature of reality itself; he views imagination as "the power to represent the real more fully and truly than it appears to the senses and in its ideal or universal character."[3]

Nineteenth-century realism had as its goal the objective representation of reality, hence it could deal only with those aspects of reality that are external and circumstantial. The inner experience of man is now accepted as being no less "real" than the world of actions. Thus today we have a more complex view of reality, which naturally requires other means of expression than objective realism.

Employing the analytic methods of science, psychology attempts to understand the nature of emotional disturbance and conflict in the human personality. The casebooks which result from psychological investigation may provide authors with models for complex fictional characters, but often the process runs in the opposite direction, with the scientist learning from literature. The special sensitivity of the creative artist and his intuition enable him to anticipate the psychologist and the psychiatrist in the accurate depiction of man's hidden needs and anxieties. Freud himself acknowledged science's debt to art when, at his seventieth birthday celebration, he asserted, "The poets and philosophers before me discovered the unconscious. What I discovered was the scientific method by which the unconscious can be studied."[4]

More than any other Mexican author, Amparo Dávila seems compelled to write on themes of mental alienation. In nearly all her stories she submerges the reader in a world that defies rational explanation. Private and haunting, it is nevertheless our real world as viewed by a deranged mind. The modern expression of that traditional literary form, the tale of terror, is well illustrated in the works of this author. Formerly, the sensation of terror was aroused by the objective recounting of supernatural incursions into the real world or of terrible physical cruelties being inflicted upon some innocent victim. Today's horror story, by contrast, is subjective and intensely personal. While it is true that for modern man increased knowledge of the material world has effectively displaced the supernatural, elucidation of the intricate functioning of the human mind remains uncertain. "El misterio está en nosotros," observed Jean Mistler with reference to the subjective tales of terror by E. T. A. Hoffmann. "El misterio está en nosotros y, cuando el vértigo nos atrae hacia el abismo, éste se oculta en lo más profundo de nuestra personalidad. . . . No hay otras visiones que los sueños y las alucinaciones, ni hay otro Demonio que la Locura."[5]

The study of psychology has produced a new kind of terror, which has been described vividly as "the nightmare country between sanity and madness; the pressure of mind upon living mind, and the lonely horror of the dark places of the soul."[6] This is not the relatively simple terror of a ghost story, but that deeper anguish experienced when one feels helpless and trapped, defenseless against some indefinable menace. As for instance, in "El huésped" (1956), where Amparo Dávila convinces the reader, without ever being explicit, of the reality of an evil presence, an actual threat to the narrator's life. Her husband had brought a "guest" home for an extended visit and then almost immediately he himself had to leave on a business trip. We never learn whether the "guest" is a person or an animal; we know only that the narrator is terrified, and gradually we too are caught up in her obsession. Perhaps there is no real threat, but we are relieved when she manages to seal the "guest" in a windowless room without food or water. She tries to ignore the desperate pounding and wailing at the door, and by the end of the second week there is only silence. The technical device of concealing the identity of the "guest" is particularly effective, since it places the reader in the same situation as the narrator, who does not understand the reason for her own terror. If we can give a shape to our fears, if we can see our problem clearly and objectively, then a way can be found to overcome it. The narrator succeeds only in locking her problem away and ignoring it; the author allows the reader to do no better.

In the stories of Amparo Dávila, psychic reality replaces that of the external world and, in order to create this special environment for the reader, unusual narrative techniques are required. The concept of time, for instance, may become the predominant structural device as in "Tiempo destrozado" (1959). Generally in literature, the flow of time is designed to impose order upon life, to simplify reality by selecting and constructing events according to a structure of causation. The artificial ordering of events in literature does not follow the strict chronological time that we suppose governs the real world. Yet it is only our body that is subject to the constraint of clock-measured time; past, present, and future exist together in the mind, though they can be differentiated when necessary, if the mind is sound. The story "Tiempo destrozado" consists of six unconnected episodes having nothing in common except that they apparently involve the same narrator-protagonist. Each episode is a profusion of symbolic dream-images arranged in uncertain sequence; each is a personal situation that develops into an anguished nightmare. No attempt is made by the author to give a principle of coherence in the episodes—they are simply juxtaposed. One element alone is constant: the point of view of the distressed and persecuted narrator observing herself at different stages of life, simultaneously. Referring to the autobiographical content of her writings, Amparo Dávila has explained that

> al tocar el tema de la locura no lo hago por moda, pose, ni mucho menos elección, de igual manera que no se elige nacer hombre, mujer o pájaro. Yo sencillamente hablo del clima que me tocó habitar y observar, de la atmósfera en que he vivido y padecido siempre. Quiero y puedo confesar que nunca he conocido el equilibrio ni la cordura, nací y he vivido en el clima del absurdo y del desencantamiento, por eso mis personajes siempre van o vienen de ahí.
>
> No creo en la literatura hecha a base de la inteligencia pura o la sola imaginación, yo creo en la literatura vivencial, ya que esto, la vivencia, es lo que comunica a la obra la clara sensación de lo desconocido, de lo ya vivido, la que hace que la obra perdure en la memoria y en el sentimiento, lo cual constituye su más exacta belleza y su fuerza interior.[7]

One reason why pathological experience has long obsessed the artist is the possible cathartic effect of embodying his personality disturbances in writing. By setting them down as objects of contemplation he may be able to free himself from their tyranny. Moreover, the artist, and especially the writer, is better able than most people to be articulate about his inner state and thus to communicate the nuances of emotion and thought that torment him. The intuitive representation of experienced symptoms can yield insights into the nature of the neurosis. Still it is important to remember that what the writer creates is primarily a work of art and not a case history: he may write for himself, for his friends, or for the general reading public, but he does not consciously write for the psychologist or the psychiatrist.

Another story by Amparo Dávila, "Final de una lucha" (1959), is an excellent example of the artistic rendering of an inner conflict. The protagonist, Durán, begins to doubt his own existence when, walking along the street one day, he actually sees himself together with a beautiful girl. Durán recognizes the smell of her perfume and realizes that she is Lilia, a girl with whom he was once in love, but who had despised him for his poverty. As he follows them he recalls the turbulent affair which nearly destroyed his sanity. It is with a certain pleasure that Durán notes how the man—his double—is treating Lilia very roughly, just as he himself had so often wanted to do. When they enter a house, Durán follows them determined to end this nightmare. He must discover whether it is he who really exists or the other man. Through the door he hears Lilia being beaten. The room is in darkness and Lilia's dead body is lying on the floor. Durán and his counterpart struggle violently for a long while. Eventually, Durán emerges from the building looking around furtively to see whether he is being observed.

The artistic elaboration of the story is remarkable. Well-integrated flashbacks in the mind of the protagonist provide the necessary background information. When the author describes Durán as being habitually insecure, she is preparing the reader for the appearance of the double and the attendant atmosphere of mystery and unreality. At the end we are not sure if Durán has actually killed someone or if the whole drama took place in his mind, a complex hallucination triggered by the smell of a particular brand of perfume with distressing associations. In either case, Durán has been plunged back into an agonizing conflict that he had mistakenly supposed resolved when he married a quiet, steady girl and took an undemanding job in a bank.

"Música concreta" (1964), the title story of Amparo Dávila's second collection, also has as its subject the tenuous line between sanity and madness. The story begins in everyday reality when Sergio meets his former sweetheart Marcela on the street and is shocked to see how haggard she looks. They go to a restaurant and she explains that she has not been able to sleep well for weeks because her husband Luis is having an affair. Marcela describes the other woman as having a deep hoarse voice, a head that appears to be fastened directly to her shoulders, a face too large for her short stature and with cold, unexpressive eyes—the same eyes as a certain toad which sits croaking outside Marcela's window night after night. In fact Marcela is convinced that the toad actually is the woman in another form and that she has come to attack her. Sergio reassures Marcela but he cannot stop thinking about her problem, and when she telephones him days later, hysterically insisting that the toad has tried to kill her, he decides to involve himself directly on Marcela's behalf. He goes to the woman's address resolved to persuade her to give up the affair. While waiting at her door, he hears strange noises like *musique concrète* coming from within. As Sergio talks to the woman, the sound becomes deafening but, oddly, she appears not to notice it. Suddenly he is struck by her undeniable resemblance to a toad, and he takes up a pair of scissors and stabs her over and over again until her croaking ceases.

We see in this story how the theme of metempsychosis is treated in literature today. Like other supernatural phenomena, the passing of souls is represented as having reality only in the mind of those involved in the delusion. When trying to console Marcela, Sergio had suggested that she was simply confusing reality and fantasy: "A veces uno sin querer—dice Sergio—, sin darse cuenta, mezcla la realidad y la fantasía y las funde, se deja atrapar en su maraña y se deja abandonar a lo absurdo, es como irse de viaje hacia una ciudad que nunca ha existido."[8] It is ironic that Sergio, who believed he had such a firm hold on reality, should eventually fall victim to his own proposition. The author prepares us for this possibility by indicating both his physical state of fatigue and the extremely close relation he formerly had with Marcela: "Habían estado todo ese tiempo tan cerca uno del otro que nunca se le ocurrió preguntarse qué clase de afecto los unía. Marcela era como una parte de él mismo."[9] Other Mexican stories of induced psychosis—e.g., "Desdoblamiento" (1959) by Alberto Bonifaz Nuño, and "El escorpión al acecho" (1960) by Carlos Valdés—by contrast are arbitrary and improbable; they are self-conscious rhetorical exercises, concerned more with formal paradoxes and irony than with the interpretation of reality as viewed by an estranged personality.

The theme of the human double or *Doppelgänger* is traditional in literature, extending back to the ancient Egyptians. During the Romantic period of European literature it was a commonplace for the hero or the villain to come face to face with an exact replica of himself. This *alter ego* often was symbolic of his conscience, his soul or his destiny. In the first chapter of the present study, this theme was considered with the supernatural properties attributed to the human image reflected in mirrors; in the third chapter, whimsical treatments of the inner struggle between different aspects of the self were discussed. The fragmenting of the human personality is recognized as a psychoneurotic reaction to uncontrollable anxiety. In order to seal off disturbing parts of the personality, a totally new identity may be assumed or the personality may break up into dissociated segments existing in a relatively autonomous way. "Conócete a ti mismo" (1964) by Jaime Cardeña is an account of a victim of acute neurotic anxiety, the cause of which he does not know. In an attempt to recover his customary peace of mind, he takes a holiday at Puerto Vallarta, but when he returns home the problem is more intense than ever. He suffers hallucinations of having spiders on the curtains and is on the verge of psychosis. Still he struggles to understand—hence the Socratic injunction of the title. He becomes convinced that there is another presence in the house with him. When he hears footsteps approach the door, he knows that he must open it and face whatever is there. He is weak and terrified, but he does manage to open the door, and there, in the darkness, he discerns a shape. He can make out its eyes, then the face: it is himself.

The subject is treated quite differently by Salvador Elizondo in "La puerta" (1966), where a woman in an asylum has a recurring nightmare that she approaches a large, locked door at the end of a corridor. She wants to open it, but she is afraid of finding her own corpse there. Each time when she is about to open it, she is set upon by dogs or the doctors restrain her. Then one grey afternoon she feels compelled to walk that corridor, to grasp the bronze doorknob and submit herself to the transcendental encounter. She opens the door and in the darkness she sees her own face smiling at her, but with a trickle of blood running from her mouth and down her chin.

Apparently, the door itself and what lies beyond it symbolize different realities for the two authors and the two patients. For Cardeña it seems to represent the critical stage in the process of psychotherapy—where the patient develops insight into his personality and his motives. In Elizondo's story, the doorway appears to lead to the final mystery: death. Both authors, nevertheless, are portraying dissociation as it is experienced from within, the pathological fear and the irremediable solitude of the disordered personality. Unfortunately, Cardeña fails to involve the reader's emotions; his account is too cool and detached. Elizondo, on the other hand, being a true artist, makes the reader share the emotions and delusions of his character. Perhaps the difference is attributable partly to the authors' opposing points of view: both have evidently attempted to turn their psychoanalytic experience into literature but, whereas Jaime Cardeña is a practicing psychiatrist, Salvador Elizondo's personal experience with treatment of mental illness has been as a patient.

By means of the study of dreams and hallucinations, the surrealist artist seeks a clearer awareness of the world. He tries to approximate that freedom of the creative imagination exhibited by children and the insane. It seems that one must realize the ambiguous nature of all things to appreciate the true relationship between man and the universe, and to this end the surrealist cultivates an art dictated by the unconscious; the false logical structure of reality is supplanted by unexpected associations, secret correspondences which the mind cannot grasp and which only the emotions can assimilate. In his *Manifeste du surréalisme* (1924), the chief spokesman of surrealism, André Breton, declared his belief in "the future transmutation of those two seemingly contradictory states, dream and reality, into a sort of absolute reality, a super-reality, so to speak."[10] Enlarging upon the same idea in the *Second manifeste du surréalisme* (1929), he stated the ambition of surrealist activity as being to determine that "certain point in the mind from which life and death, the real and the imaginary, the past and future, what is communicable and what is incommunicable, the high and the low, cease to be perceived as contradictory."[11] As an integrated movement, surrealism came to an end with the Second World War; but it continues to exercise an influence on the many artists who aspire to go beyond aesthetic achievements and to gain a metaphysical knowledge of reality.

Amparo Dávila fuses different states of reality in "El jardín de las tumbas" (1964) in such a way that the reader's attempts to grasp any logical sense are in vain. Here it is not the technical device of omitting clock-measured time that is baffling, but rather the story's central idea. Marcos, now forty years old, is reading the diary that he wrote between the ages of nine and sixteen. Passages from the diary are interspersed among the thoughts of Marcos as he reads about the summers of his childhood spent playing in the ruins of an old monastery. He recalls ghosts he had imagined and the terror of darkness that he never overcame. Marcos concludes his reading, makes his plans for the following day and then retires for the night. In the morning he is wakened by Jacinta, his nanny. It is a summer morning in the country and he is Marcos the child. The concluding sentence:

> El niño se removió en la cama y bostezó repetidas veces, y a medida que iba despertando y su mente se empezaba a despejar, experimentaba una gran sensación de alivio al comprobar que por fortuna había pasado otra noche de espanto y ya era nuevamente de día.[12]

The child could not have dreamt about his future, since there are details that would be beyond a child's knowledge; yet he is a child and not an adult. The logical mind of the reader is left bewildered and only the emotions can respond. At every stage in the development there is perfect clarity, but when the story is considered as a whole it slips irretrievably beyond reason. Amparo Dávila's lucid prose style contributes significantly to the reader's perplexity and has led to her art being characterized as "una peculiar visión racional de lo irracional."[13]

The interpenetration of the sleeping and the waking states, the region between life and death, is treated briefly by Francisco Tario in "Mi noche" (1943) and more intensively in "Entre tus dedos helados" (1968). In the latter story the narrator is dreaming that he is accused by the police of having raped and decapitated a young girl. He pleads that he is innocent, that it is just a dream, but he soon begins to wonder whether he might be mistaken. For the dream is infinitely more real to him than that other reality that he can scarcely perceive: his parents and the doctor leaning over his bed. In the dream, a girl is making sexual advances to him, while in reality his mother is urging him to make an effort to wake up. He does wake up but the police are still with him, while, in that other dream, the doctor is shaking his head sadly and his parents are weeping. The unexpected injection of humor and eroticism, mingling pathos with comedy, death with sex, render grotesque what would otherwise have been a poignant story of a young man's transition into death.

The grotesque, resulting from the fusion of elements of horror with humor, is characteristic of surrealism, for it destroys common reality and then presents it recreated and estranged from us. The grim "black humor" of the surrealist constitutes an act of revolt against social morality and conventional norms. It is alleged that these obstruct the apprehension of true reality, which is instinctive and irrational. Especially in his early stories, published as *La noche* (1943), Francisco Tario practiced the surrealist's method of upsetting respectable society by treating morally repugnant subjects, and with irresistible humor: death is again related to sexual adventure when, in "La noche del féretro," the coffin dumps out the body of an old man and says that it prefers to pass through eternity wedded and fusing with a female corpse; mass murder by poisoning is gaily depicted in "La noche de la gallina"; and, in "La noche del loco," necrophilia.

Alfredo Cardona Peña tells what appears to be a conventional horror story in "La otra muerte" (1966), where a cataleptic, thought to be dead, is lying helpless in the morgue watching a ghoul go from corpse to corpse, sucking out the eyes of the dead. But at the critical moment he is saved, and the story is given a gratuitous macabre twist when we are informed that the ghoul, who had escaped from an asylum, was once the champion oyster eater of the Caribbean seaboard. In such stories as "León de Israel" (1960) and "Parque de diversiones" (1962), José Emilio Pacheco flaunts his rejection of his own middle-class background. The first depicts a Jewish cloth merchant named León Papilovsky, who is celebrating his birthday at the office. A French chef has been engaged to sculpt for him a huge lion from a block of ice. As León poses for a photograph, with his head in the mouth of the sculpted lion, the mouth closes and León's head is cut off. When they accuse the French chef of excessive realism in his creations, the story is revealed as symbolizing the perpetual antagonism between the artist and the philistine materialist.

"Parque de diversiones" is like a Sunday stroll through Mexico City's Chapultepec Park, but with the normal activities viewed with a satanic eye and carried to absurd extremes. In one scene a teacher shows her class around the Botanical Garden and feeds two of the children to carnivorous plants; in another a happy family picnic comes to an end when invading ants and hungry dogs devour the food and then the people. For the republication of the story in 1963 Pacheco added an episode about a children's train that usually fails to return. In those cases when it does come back the children have become frightened, resentful adults.

Perhaps Mexico's best example of grotesque humor is "La co-cinera" (1940) by Julio Torri. One reacts with disgust and uneasy laughter to this story of a superb cook who has made her employer famous in high society. Everyone raves about her exquisite dishes, until one day a child's finger is discovered in a *tamal*. Indeed she was responsible for the disappearance of many babies in the district, yet her memory is still revered by certain gastronomes, including the narrator, who regularly place flowers on her tomb.

Laughter at the expense of social convention has a liberating effect; it calls common morality into question when the accepted world view is seen to be inapplicable. On the value of "black humor" Eugène Ionesco has suggested that

> humor makes us conscious, with a free lucidity, of the tragic or desultory condition of man. . . . It is not only the critical spirit itself . . . but . . . humor is the only possibility we possess of detaching ourselves— yet only after we have surmounted, assimilated, taken cognizance of it —from our tragicomic human condition, the malaise of being. To become conscious of what is horrifying and to laugh at it is to become master of that which is horrifying. . . . Logic reveals itself in the illogicality of the absurd of which we have become aware. Laughter alone does not respect any taboo, laughter alone inhibits the creation of new anti-taboo taboos; the comic alone is capable of giving us the strength to bear the tragedy of existence. The true nature of things, truth itself, can be revealed to us only by fantasy, which is more realistic than all the realisms.[14]

Still another means of alienating the familiar outlook on life is the imaginative and irresponsible literature of verbal nonsense. In Mexico, however, pure nonsense literature is rare. There is no writer who combines a rich exuberant verbal imagination with extravagant free association in the manner of a Lewis Carroll or an Edward Lear. "El epitalamio de Onésimo Segundo" (1962) by Jaime Cardeña is an ingenious jumble of paradoxes and contradictions beginning with the birth (on the Day of the Dead) of Onésimo Segundo (his parents' third child), and ending when, at the age of forty-five and despite perfect health, "se juevó un muertes 13 de diciembre."[15] The story is manifestly absurd, but there is nevertheless an orderly unfolding of the events. For the surrealist, the main purpose of pure nonsense would be to upset all logic, to destroy the false sense of security that language gives. The only Mexican author with the requisite audacity is Francisco Tario whose "La noche de los genios raros" (1943), for instance, is an extended dialogue composed of the neologisms and non sequiturs that one associates with the total disorientation of a psychotic break with reality:

I.- (Con el paraguas alado.) ¡Tú!
II.- (Sin paraguas.) ¡Yo!
I.- ¡Yo también!
II.- Subjetivamente.
I.- ¿Vas al teatro?. . . .
II.- Ve.
I.- Justo. Me quedo.
II.- ¿Tan tarde?
I.- No hay hora.
II.- Sólo números romanos. . . .
I.- (Infinitamente mordaz.) Y papagayos.[16]

Ideally, on being liberated from their ordinary context, words take on a new and autonomous value in a poetic reality totally created by the author. Again the source of creativity is the unconscious mind, with free association as the most reliable means of access.

The surrealists began with the declaration that art was failing to provide a completely truthful representation of the world, inasmuch as it ignored dreams and the dark region of the unconscious. Yet instead of elaborating a wider concept of reality, they become lost in their descent into the deepest part of the human being. In limiting their attention exclusively to exploring the subliminal mind, the surrealists themselves present a deficient view of life. The unconscious realities make up only one part of human experience and, while perception may be individual, there are important social and philosophical concepts that govern the conscious level of experience, the world in which we live day by day.

⬦⬦⬦⬦⬦⬦⬦

Literature that endeavors to record the workings of the unconscious mind presents the familiar themes of folklore in a new light. In less sophisticated ages, man's fears and anxieties were naively expressed in tales of the supernatural, where there was no doubt or mystery—the manifestation from the spirit world, whether ghost, monster or demon, was portrayed as objective and real. For the modern writer, supernatural explanations are seldom satisfactory. He is more likely to want to show the obsession of his characters as precisely and faithfully as possible. Being engaged in the writing of imaginative literature, he attempts to explore hidden areas of reality, not simply to create an uncanny effect. The modern counterpart of folklore's objective supernatural fantasy, then, is the subjective, intuitive and emotional perception of inner conflict. The menace in Amparo Dávila's story "El huésped," for example, is indefinable and yet it provokes a mental state of terror; the *Doppelgänger* of her "Final de una lucha" is not gratuitous, but might be accounted for as dissociation of the personality brought about by extreme anxiety and, as with the transmigration of the soul in "Música concreta," the delusion is only in the mind of the protagonist. All the same, the interpretation of such works is never quite clear and unequivocal, and the reader must participate with more than his intellect if he is to appreciate their significance.

The imaginative stories discussed in the present chapter, particularly those of Amparo Dávila and Salvador Elizondo, typify what Jung calls the "visionary" mode of artistic creation, as opposed to the "psychological" mode:

> In dealing with the psychological mode of artistic creation, we never need ask ourselves what the material consists of or what it means. But this question forces itself upon us as soon as we come to the visionary mode of creation. We are astonished, taken aback, confused, put on our guard or even disgusted—and we demand commentaries and explanations. We are reminded in nothing of everyday, human life, but rather of dreams, night-time fears and the dark recesses of the mind that we sometimes sense with misgiving.[17]

Whether the vision derives from the personal experiences of the artist is unimportant for its consideration as a work of art. Indeed these authors do not present mere clinical case-studies of mental disorder, but rather moving, intuitive insights into the unconscious psychic life of man.

CHAPTER VI

Expressionism

At about the time of the First World War, the French cubist painters and the Italian futurists were celebrating the new mechanistic view of reality, which they reduced to its fundamental geometric forms. But in Germany art was following a different direction in reaction against a crass, positivistic, ultra-mechanized world. The Germans were destroying form and color emotionally in order to discover the underlying universal significance, the non-rational and spiritual values in life. These "expressionist" artists expressed their troubled psychological states through tortured figures and landscapes; the images and forms of the outer world were transformed in response to inner feelings. As described by Sir Herbert Read, the expressionist "is openly in revolt against the conventions of the normal conception of reality and is endeavoring to create a vision of reality more strictly in accordance with his own emotional reactions to experience."[1]

Historically, the expressionist movement was at the height of its influence in the first years of the 1920s, not only in painting but also in literature and especially in the theater. Yet expressionist techniques and attitudes continue to survive as the basis and inspiration of a great deal of contemporary art:

> Modern expressionism in its enormous proliferation has been—and still is—the noisy, seething experimental laboratory for Western man's aesthetic models for selfhood in a world in which the older patterns have been discredited. It has tried everything, sometimes borrowing

from the latest currents of thought and fashion, and sometimes striking out on its own. . . .

As mirror and recapitulator of life, modern art has exhibited a great variety of interpretations of the outcome and condition of Western man and his civilization. Modern art was first to put on exhibit the nihilism, the vacuity, the despair, and the deathly mechanization and de-personification of the existing man in our time. One has to have experienced what Sartre calls "nausea" to know the honesty of certain modern expressions. In much of this art, there is all the explosion, the dismemberment of the human soul, and the distortion which anyone who cares to look, can easily find in our troubled world. If in this art the object of perception and the whole world of such objects have fallen apart in violence, so also has the mind and soul of modern man.[2]

Expressionist art is highly personal and, being aimed at appreciation by the few, it is implicitly antisocial. In Spanish America, critics tend to associate these works of imagination with fantasies and with detective and adventure stories—all of which they censure as de-humanized "literatura de avestruz"[3] in which the writer evades his unquestionable obligation to denounce social injustice. According to one of these critics, "es literatura . . . exhibicionista . . . para minorías ociosas, frívolas y snob."[4] Most writers enjoy being frivolous occasionally, no doubt, and for this many readers are grateful. A character created by Francisco Tario expresses this preference:

La literatura realista no me interesa; me abruma. . . . No soy de los que admiran a un literato porque exponga con precisión algebraica la forma en que yo, mi padre, mi hijo y los hijos de mis hijos suelan llevarse un pitillo a la boca o introducirse un supositorio en el ano.[5]

Indeed, if lyric poetry is granted a place of honor in literature, may the narrator not provide us with a refuge from oppressive circumstances —an imaginary world for the recreation of the spirit, the regeneration of the soul?

At any rate, the disrepute of pure, capricious fantasy usually is extended to include as well literature of the imagination, which in fact does not avoid human conflicts, though it treats them with symbolic techniques. The complexities of existence cannot be fully apprehended from any single perspective and every artist may consider his original perception to be true and realistic. In the words of Alain Robbe-Grillet, "Tous les écrivains pensent être réalistes. Aucun jamais ne se prétend abstrait, illusioniste, chimérique, fantaisiste, faussaire . . . ."[6] Certain periods of history are better represented by an intuitive vision than by strict logical realism. The destruction and madness of the First World War, for example, engendered the violent anti-art of Dada, from which surrealism emerged. Similarly, in an age when science is based largely on abstract computations about imagined molecular structures, in an age characterized by an over-whelming chaos of bewildering information, modern man has sought to express his predicament in the existential cast of absurdist litera-ture. Now—as then—man's fettered spirit finds release through vio-lence and fanaticism. Now—as then—revelation is sought in the human unconscious, in the self-induced hallucination, and once again rationalism is declared bankrupt.

During the decade between 1950 and 1960 a heated polemic took place in Mexico, which involved everyone concerned with the arts. In 1963 Rosario Castellanos recalled the controversy:

> Hasta hace muy poco tiempo no era posible leer una página de prosa narrativa sin preguntarse inmediatamente quién de los antagonistas era el modelo del autor: Juan Rulfo o Juan José Arreola. Si sus personajes deliraban de hambre y de sufrimiento o si se entregaban al libre juego de la imaginación. Si nos ponía enfrente una pétrea esfinge campesina o nos dibujaba en el aire una figura ligera e inaprehensible. Si nos en-tregaba una víscera sangrante o una piedra cuidadosamente pulida. Si se afiliaba, en fin, al realismo mágico o a la fantasía pura.[7]

But it is time the prevailing opinion which takes Arreola as represent-ing this category of superficial and gratuitous literature were challenged.

Perhaps the most obvious features of Arreola's stories are their stylistic elegance and the extravagance of their action, either of which would be enough to set them apart from the course of the Mexican narrative so long subject to evaluation according to ethical and not aesthetic criteria. Socialist realism values content above form, and encourages direct expression of an impersonal conception of reality. Arreola acknowledges the artist's social responsibility, but he con-tends that documentary fiction is merely a useless repetition of life and that its task could much more effectively be performed by the newspaper, radio, cinema, or television.[8]

If art is the transformation of exterior reality into aesthetic experi-ence, Arreola is the consummate artist with absolute control over the word—which is for him the material concretion of an emanation from the human soul. He rejoices in the constant accusations that he is *manierista, amanerado, filigranista, orfebre,*[9] but he rejects the se-renity of the ivory tower and specifically urges

> una lucha honda y constante en pro de la paz universal. Nadie mejor que el artista para emprenderla y proclamarla. Porque ser artista, no es una disculpa para la inacción, sino más bien un compromiso grave y profundo que no debe ser eludido.[10]

Instead of directing his criticism against obvious national symp-toms—poverty, illiteracy, and political corruption—Arreola attacks the malady at its source: the moral conscience of the individual. His story "Informe de Liberia" (1959) deals with unborn children who refuse to enter this world. "Flash" (1955) reports on a mad scientist whose patriotic invention, an atomic "absorber," has ingested a large number of his fellow countrymen together with the railway train in which they were traveling. "En verdad os digo" (1952) presents us with another scientist whose power of invention is greater than his sense of morality. He earns a fortune with an ingenious project to construct a machine capable of passing a camel through the eye of a needle. "Baby H.P." (1952) is a sort of Leyden jar fitted with a harness, which is designed to convert a baby's tremendous energy into electricity. The idea seems both grotesque and frivolous, but at bottom it is quite serious. What Arreola wants to suggest is, first, that the baby could electrocute itself (physical annihilation) and, second, that blind utilitarianism will annihilate man spiritually.

Such a depreciation of moral values necessarily implies the failure of religion and, in "De L'Osservatore" (1962), we have a notice from the Vatican newspaper advising us briefly that, at the beginning of our Era, Saint Peter's keys were lost in the suburbs of the Roman Empire. The finder is asked kindly to deliver them to the reigning Pope because for more than fifteen hundred years no one has been able to enter the Kingdom of Heaven. The concrete indications of the period (more than fifteen centuries ago), the setting (in the suburbs of the Roman Empire), and the religious context when taken together suggest Constantine, who established himself in Byzantium in A.D. 313. It will be recalled that, following his conversion, Constantine proclaimed Christianity the official state religion. Thus penetrating below the surface of the (apparent) caprice, we can discern some aspect of Arreola's personal vision; in this case, his conviction that, at the moment of instituting the Church, Christianity lost its validity (the keys were lost). Arreola returns to this theme in a recent story, to which he gives an English title, "Starring: All People" (1967), and which he offers in homage to Cecil B. De Mille.[11] Here the history of the world is presented as an incomplete and mediocre movie that failed with both the public and the critics. The star actor, Jesus Christ, reveals to us in an interview that he is dying to go back to remake the film and give it a happy ending, but his father is still withholding his permission.

Arreola's philosophy of life is most adequately expressed in "El guardagujas" (1952), a Kafkaesque story concerning a fantastic railway system with only some sections completed, but where it is possible to buy tickets for any destination. No one knows what trains are running or where they are going. At any moment a train might arrive at the edge of an abyss where no bridge has been constructed. In such a case, the passengers dismantle the train and carry the parts to the other side, there to rebuild it and continue their journey. According to Arreola, this is what life is like: a series of absurd chance occurrences to which every man should surrender himself. In the same way, the moles of "Topos" (1952) yield to the attraction of death, leaping into the holes that lead to the fiery center of the earth. "La caverna" (1952), where one wanders in fear and trembling, is a vision of the final unknowable nothingness. But even as we are drawn to the universality of death, so we seek to lose our individuality in woman. Hence "Topos" and "La caverna" can also be interpreted satisfactorily as symbolic of the sexual experience.

For the existentialist, nothing matters more than the authenticity of his choices and the personal relationships he achieves. The natural hope that through sex a complete communion is possible becomes an obsession in Arreola. He confesses that "la percepción de la mujer . . . ha sido el *leitmotiv* de mi existencia."[12] Recently he composed a list of the women who have played a decisive role in his life, not just lovers but also teachers, relatives, and writers. The list stands at seventy-two names. On the subject of woman, Arreola has always expressed himself with bitterness, an attitude which his one great love affair (1953-58) served only to reinforce.

"El soñado" (1949) is a narration in the first person by what seems to be an imaginary or unborn child, but is in fact the monstrous thing that two people engender just by living together. It is not literally a child but a presence, an ill feeling, an animosity, an indifference. Arreola does not conceal his resentment and disillusion. Reluctantly he acknowledges the impossibility of love, but he attaches part of the blame to man for he falsifies the nature of woman. "Una mujer amaestrada" (1955) gives us a tragic vision of marriage: a mountebank grotesquely exhibiting his wife to the public and making her perform clumsy dances and feats of simple arithmetic as if she were a trained bear so that the spectators will share his opinion of this marvelous woman. The female plastic robots of "Anuncio" (1962) and "Parábola del trueque" (1955) represent woman as a mere tool for the sexual satisfaction of man. But it is woman herself who accepts all these conflicting roles that man invents. At one moment she is asked to be a goddess, then she is a maid, then a devil, and then a mother. . . . Arreola is not anti-feminist and his conclusions distress him since they blasphemously attack his sacred concept of woman, which is more or less as follows:

> Necesito abrazar en la mujer el árbol de la vida, creer que estoy ligado a la vida universal, que ya no hay individuación, que la mujer es, en este

momento, la puerta de escape hacia el todo. La mujer que nos trajo de la universalidad a la individuación, es también la puerta del paraíso. Reingreso de la individualidad al todo. Por eso en el amor existe ese perderse, dejarse derivar como en un río.[13]

It is worth noting parenthetically that Arreola is overcoming his disillusionment with woman. He sees the history of civilization thus far as characterized by its masculinity and he considers it a failure. The only possible salvation for humanity, he now believes, is through woman and a new feminine orientation in life.

Because Arreola's work is full of humor and irony, he has been regarded as a jester interested only in novelty and in amusing or scandalizing the reader. Indeed Arreola is a formalist and a virtuoso of the Spanish language, but almost never is he trivial or gratuitous. On the contrary, his themes are profoundly human. He employs elements of his own personal drama to express, in fragments, a vision of man's existence. Arreola's concise style together with his intuitive technique produce incomprehension on the part of the public. His meaning is never obvious or easily accessible, but it always exists—between the lines.

The famous polemic, then, which arose from the indignation and outrage surrounding the publication of his first works misrepresented Arreola's position, but it did serve to vitalize Mexican letters for more than a decade. The *arreolistas* proclaimed the supremacy of art, an essentially intuitive faculty, over all national and political considerations. Their mentor taught respect for aesthetic values and demonstrated how literature could be raised above the merely regional and circumstantial.

The imaginative works of Carlos Fuentes have been regarded with similar bewilderment and hostility. The themes which Fuentes treats are more acceptable than those favored by Arreola, but his expressionist techniques are enough to scandalize conservative Mexican criticism. The first book that Fuentes published—a collection of short stories entitled *Los días enmascarados* (1954)—was composed entirely of such controversial material. One of these stories, "El que inventó la pólvora," tells of a strange sort of plague that sweeps across the nation. The narrator suggests that Aldous Huxley was probably to blame for the disaster simply because in an essay he had quoted an American engineer as saying that anyone who builds a skyscraper that lasts more than forty years is a traitor to the construction industry. One morning, as the narrator is stirring his breakfast coffee, the spoon suddenly disintegrates. A week later he finds that all his utensils and those of his friends have similarly become useless and must be replaced. Factories increase their production to the limit in order to meet the enormous demand for silverware. Before long, shoes, furniture, automobiles, clothing, and books too are crumbling, and the entire population goes to work in the factories in a vain attempt to replace the goods as fast as they become unserviceable. In this way, Fuentes satirizes both materialism and the concept of dynamic obsolescence that characterizes the capitalist economies. By exaggerating the aspect of consumption, he expresses with emphasis his disdain for the economic theory.

Carlos Fuentes does not compose idle fantasies, but impassioned protests against bourgeois society, works that he prefers to term "symbolic realism":

> Aspiro a expresarme mediante un realismo que sólo puede ser comprensible y totalizante a través de símbolos, entendidos en su acepción más clara. . . . Lo alegórico se refiere a una tabla de verdades preestablecidas que la alegoría no hace sino parafrasear. Desligada de su tabla de mandamientos, de verdades *a priori*, la alegoría no tiene sentido. Por tales razones rechazo la alegoría como expresión literaria. Creo que es una forma de conformismo, de mixtificación. El símbolo, en cambio, es una referencia a algo que está en duda, a algo que se busca. Es un intento de encontrar la verdad.[14]

In whatever he writes, Fuentes reveals a passionate involvement with issues of political, social, and economic justice. His impatience with professional politicians is made clear in the essay-like story "En defensa de la Trigolibia" (1954), which begins as follows:

> La Trigolibia es el valor supremo de los Nusitanios. Cuando los Nusitanios se trigolibiaron de los Terribrios, lo primero que hicieron fue proclamar un Acta de Trigolibia y una Declaración de los Trigolibios del Hombre. Inmediatamente, colocaron ambos documentos en una vitrina y cobraron diez trigolíbidos por entrar a verlos. Organizados en Trigolíbica Trigoliba, los Nusitanios procedieron a elegir un Gran Trigolibio de la Trigolíbica.[15]

Fuentes himself has said of this story that it is "una sátira sobre la retórica contemporánea. No posee otro sentido. Esta retórica tiende a reducir las cosas al absurdo."[16] But it seems fairly clear that the "Trigolibia," so disputed in this extended play on words, refers to the ideals of democracy and freedom. Perhaps one could go still further, with some confidence, and suppose that Nusitania represents that United States ("Nusitania se convirtió en el país más poderoso y trigolíbico del mundo, y cuando fue necesario, mandó tropas a todas partes a fin de defender con la Trigolibia y hacer al mundo trigolíbico para la Trigolibia"[17]) and Tropereta, the countries of Latin America ("Los hombres de Tropereta se vieron obligados a no llevar amistad

más que con los de Nusitania, y a venderles sólo a ellos sus tro-
peranos, troperocos y troperóleos''[18]).

Also included among Fuentes's first stories, "Letanía de la orquídea" (1954) is a bizarre, almost surrealistic piece set in Panama. A
man named Muriel is surprised to find that overnight a beautiful
orchid has emerged at the base of his spine. Although the flower
causes him some inconvenience (such as the need to cut a hole for it in
his trousers), he is delighted with it. That night he dances with
abandon, while everyone stands admiring his flower. The idea occurs
to him that if he were to cut it off, another might grow, and he could
sell them. But when he removes the flower, a rough wooden stake
appears in its place and begins to drive upwards between his legs,
through his intestines and into his heart, splitting him in two. In order
to interpret this story, one has to recognize the importance of the
setting. For, like Muriel, Panama sacrificed a part of itself for an
expected commercial gain and was left divided in two and destroyed.

The United States has an enormous impact on nearly all aspects
of life in Mexico, as well as in Panama and the rest of Latin America.
And because the practical necessity of foreign capital investment is
difficult to reconcile with feelings of intense nationalism, the United
States finds itself encouraged to help develop modern industry in
Latin America and, at the same time, criticized for doing so. The
equivocal nature of the Mexican attitude towards the United States is
illustrated by Rafael Solana in "La epilitia" (1953), which he wrote
specifically for publication in the first issue of Siempre!, Mexico's
outstanding political magazine. The story's title refers to an epidemic
that is reported in Italy. The symptoms of the disease are like those of
leprosy, but its unique feature is that it attacks only marble statues.
For no reason at all the government decides that the American tourists
in Italy are to blame for it. Ironically, the consideration of whether the
tourists should all be executed in the Colosseum has to be interrupted
because the officials wish to attend a ball that night at the Embassy of
the United States.

Satire of national politics can also be found in Mexican fiction,
but usually it is expressed in an oblique and ambiguous manner. An
example is "El lunático" (1961) by Florencio Sánchez Cámara, in
which the author's message is artfully concealed. A simple situation
is viewed from the moon through a telescope: a moribund dog with its
flesh turned green and with blood coming from its mouth; and also a
dainty pet dog from which a gold-colored leash runs to the hand of a
dark figure. The action is minimal: a thoughtless movement of the
hand pulls the fancy little dog onto the other one, which despite its
feeble state, attacks and kills the pet. In its formal and stylistic re-

finement, this miniature follows the line of Mariano Silva y Aceves, Julio Torri, and Juan José Arreola. Only after repeated close reading and consideration of the color symbolism does it become apparent that this beautiful text is really an ironic accusation against Mexican government and business interests, that it represents the Mexican people as being sacrificed by local scoundrels but ultimately in the interest of foreign exploiters.

Occasionally, however, someone dares to satirize government policies or practices more openly. One story of this type is especially worth mentioning: "Ataque al amanecer" (1968), by a young writer called Gustavo Santaella Cortés. Although deficient in artistic quality, the the story is prophetic and markedly outspoken. Early one Sunday morning the government declares that a state of emergency exists in the nation. Mexico, it seems, is under threat of imminent attack by an unspecified foreign power. Immediate evacuation of the capital is to begin with young men between the ages of fourteen and twenty and all teachers and students of the University of Mexico, the National Polytechnical Institute, and the National Teachers' College. They are transported to a secret underground city prepared by the government in the remote region bounded by Oaxaca, Puebla and Guerrero, where they are to be confined permanently. Thus isolated from society they will be allowed to continue their studies, while on the surface all institutions of higher learning are to be abolished and the buildings used for the storage of corn and grain. In a television address to the nation, the president announces that the emergency has passed and that the people are once again safe from foreign aggression and the disruptive radical students. The reader is left to conclude that it is rather the safety of the government that has been assured, and only temporarily. The students and teachers have been forced underground, literally, but they are not destroyed; the revolution is merely postponed. This story was published in a Mexico City newspaper on Sunday, July 21, 1968—only one day before the incident in the National Polytechnical Institute which triggered the student uprising that eventually was terminated by the deliberate slaughter by government troops of between two hundred and three hundred protesters in the Plaza de las Tres Culturas on October 2, 1968.

The efficient social and economic development of the Spanish-American republics has been hampered ever since the colonial period by a well-established tradition of nepotism. The creation of jobs for relatives of relatives of those in power naturally results in an excessive number of public functionaries and an elaborate bureaucratic structure. For members of the general public, the labyrinthine process of forms, documents, delays and bribes effectively obstructs their access to higher officials. In "Maniobras palaciegas" (1960), Eduardo Lizalde tells of one whose office is so well protected against intrusion that years pass before it is discovered that he has been displaced by his personal chauffeur.

The theme of alienation of the individual as associated with bureaucratization is strikingly portrayed by Eugenio Trueba in "Antesala" (1951). The protagonist of this story waits interminably to be granted an audience by a certain public official. From time to time the employees in the outer office are replaced, perhaps by periodic elections, but still he is not admitted. We note in this situation a parallel with Franz Kafka's enigmatic novel *Das Schloss* (1926), in which the land surveyor K. is summoned to a castle he cannot penetrate. To neither character does it ever occur to abandon the project. Trueba depicts the progressive loss of personal identity as his perfect "antesalista" begins to feel that he is coming to resemble the office furniture. In "Confesión al prójimo" (1951), Trueba carries the process a stage further with a character who learns that he scarcely exists in the estimation of his wife or of his employer. When he murders his wife and confesses the crime to the police, they dismiss him, reasoning that the murder must have been committed by someone and, since he does not exist, he must logically be innocent. In his stories, Eugenio Trueba forcefully presents the degrading fundamental absurdity of human existence, a view of modern man as castrated and impotent, estranged in a world of insincerity and impersonal forces.

The narrator of "No escondas tu cara" (1960), by Arturo Souto Alabarce, has been driven mad in an encounter with a man who wears a mask for a face. Beneath the mask there is another mask, beneath the latter yet another. The narrator attacks him and rips off mask after mask in a desperate attempt to discover his true face, but there are only masks. Perhaps inspired by the Peer Gynt legend and the image of an onion's layers being peeled away to reveal the absence of any core, Souto Alabarce has expressed a personal view of contemporary man. His charge goes beyond that commonplace of the Baroque period: namely, that people conceal their true selves. Rather the suggestion is that modern man actually has no real face; alienated in a depersonalized world, man has no clear sense of a personal identity. The possibility of salvation through love and personal integrity is implied here, and again by Ernesto Ramos Meza in his dream-like novel, *La muerte de Pamilo* (1964). Pamilo is a sort of Christ who gives his life so that the multitude might regain the capacity to dream and might also discard its fraudulent values. Replete with biblical allusions, this fascinating, moralistic parable preaches idealism and satirizes demagoguery and rigid governmental bureaucracy.

Carlos Valdés has symbolized the existential human condition as he sees it in "La calle aún es nuestra" (1961). He evokes an enigmatic situation involving two hungry tramps reminiscent of the characters in Samuel Beckett's *Waiting for Godot* (1952). An atmosphere of mystery is created, as they walk aimlessly along a deserted street on a rainy night. One of the tramps is trying to get away from the other who pesters him incessantly for money he does not have, while both are attempting to elude the police patrols. They are pathetic and trapped, without hope unless they come to realize the contingency of their situation, their need for each other, and finally to accept an ethic of human responsibility that will transcend their nihilism. We observed earlier how Juan José Arreola embodied his view of existence in the absurd railway system of "El guardagujas." The metaphor of the preposterous journey has likewise been employed by the *estridentista* writer Arqueles Vela and, more recently, by Mauricio Gómez Mayorga in "El viaje redondo" (1929) and "La navegación" (1956), respectively. Both men were inspired on long ocean voyages between Mexico and Europe to represent the ship as the world in miniature, a bizarre microcosm governed by arbitrary and unappealable laws.

Certainly the most dramatic representation of the human predicament is "En la playa" (1964) by Salvador Elizondo, a pursuit situation from which there is no escape. An unnamed fat man is shown running with difficulty along a sandy beach, trying to escape from a rifleman who is drawing ever nearer in a boat rowed mechanically by two mulattos. The hunter is called Van Guld, but we do not know who he is or why he is going to kill the fat man. He is completely dispassionate, while the fat man tries desperately to scramble over the dunes, sinking into the loose sand with each attempt. If he could only cross the dunes, he thinks, he might reach the trees and be safe. There is no emotion in the story except fear. The steady pace conveys the idea of fatal inexorability, which is only heightened by the frantic efforts of the fat man. Elizondo paints the situation with bold expressionist colors: the sea is calm, a stroke of blue; the beach, a golden strand; the jungle, an unattainable green ribbon visible over the dunes; the sky is clear. Death exists as a fact from which there is no escape. For modern man, the consciousness of this fact and of the cosmic insignificance of the human species has left life without any absolute meaning or purpose—in short, it is absurd:

> In a universe suddenly divested of illusions and lights, man feels an alien, a stranger. His exile is without remedy since he is deprived of the

memory of a lost home or the hope of a promised land. This divorce
between man and his life, the actor and his setting, is properly the
feeling of absurdity.[19]

The fat man in Elizondo's story, like the anguished characters of
Franz Kafka, lacks the courage to rebel against the absurd, to affirm
the self and the importance of life. If there are no absolutes, a metaphysical quest will fail to get anywhere. Man must therefore assume
the responsibility for fashioning his own essence in the consistently
scrupulous pursuit of those goals that he himself has invested with
value.

◇◇◇◇◇◇◇◇

The works treated above are not escapist fantasies, but products
of intense involvement in moral and philosophical problems of daily
life. Here reality is attacked, distorted and exaggerated for the sake of
the author's subjective, frequently apocalyptic, vision: Carlos Fuentes
issues a vigorous protest against political and social injustice; Salvador Elizondo, Eugenio Trueba and Juan José Arreola objectify their
sense of man's alienation and anguish; and Arreola expresses his
contempt for the materialism, moral debasement, hatred and confusion that he believes prevail in the modern world.

The general reading public does not readily accept or comprehend these works which, because they arise from states of despair,
anger and spiritual distress, are often deliberately and aggressively
obscure. Arreola, Fuentes, and Elizondo are not primarily concerned
with the communication of specific messages to the reader and,
notwithstanding the dream-like quality of the stories, neither do they
share the surrealist's interest in the workings of the unconscious
mind. These authors have succeeded admirably, however, in produc-
ing works of art—conceived of as creation and revelation, not as
mimesis—by symbolizing their complex emotional responses to the
conscious level of reality, and without the sacrifice of themes of social
significance.

CHAPTER VII

Magical Realism

In Germany a period of exuberant hopes for social improvement had given way by 1923 to disillusionment and cynicism. The passionate idealism and subjectivity of expressionist art was replaced by a straightforward objectivity with minutely exact techniques of description. The themes that inspired the new art were no longer vast generalities or visionary experiences, but rather the common elements of immediate reality, which were documented as the intense search for the "beyond-rational inner meaning"[1] continued, although now without the rebellious destruction of form. This interlude in German art between Expressionism and National Socialism, the so-called New Objectivity period, was characterized by "quiet exploration of the very magic of being, out of which new associative values and moods are derived."[2] The name, apparently, was coined by G. F. Hartlaub, director of the Mannheim Art Gallery at that time, in a circular letter dated May 18, 1923, in which he asked German museum directors, art dealers, and critics for the names and addresses of artists who might be invited to take part in an exhibition of such post-expressionist objective paintings and graphics. The letter begins with a description of the tendency:

> I wish in the autumn to arrange a medium-sized exhibition of paintings and prints, which could be given the designation "Die neue Sachlichkeit." I am interested in bringing together representative works of those artists who in the last ten years have been neither impressionistically relaxed nor expressionistically abstract, who have

devoted themselves exclusively neither to external sense impressions, nor to pure inner construction. I wish to exhibit those artists who have remained unswervingly faithful to positive palpable reality, or who have become faithful to it once more.[3]

Although the exhibition was planned for September of 1923, technical difficulties delayed its production until the summer of 1925. It was as the subtitle of a book by the art critic Franz Roh on New Objectivity and the Mannheim exhibition that the term "magical realism" was introduced.[4]

The earliest appearance of the term in Spanish-American literary criticism is due to the Venezuelan Arturo Uslar Pietri, who, writing in 1948 on the subject of the short story in Venezuela during the last twenty years, affirmed that

> lo que vino a predominar en el cuento y a marcar su huella de una manera perdurable fue la consideración del hombre como misterio en medio de los datos realistas. Una adivinación poética o una negación poética de la realidad. Lo que a falta de otra palabra podría llamarse un realismo mágico.[5]

It will be noted that the idea of man as a mystery in a realistic setting is consistent with the original connotation of "magical realism" as found in German art criticism. But when Uslar Pietri extends it to include stories in which reality is poetically negated, he prepares the way for indiscriminate confusion with the whole realm of fantasy.

Except for Alejo Carpentier, whose conception of "lo real maravilloso" (formulated in 1949) as a phenomenon peculiar to the New World will be discussed presently, the next writer after Uslar Pietri to speak of "magical realism" is the Cuban Marxist critic José Antonio Portuondo. For Portuondo, the term is simply a pejorative designation as he uses it to denounce the works of the American authors Arthur Miller, Norman Mailer, Truman Capote, and Tennessee Williams, and those of the Spanish-Americans Eduardo Mallea, María Luisa Bombal, José Revueltas, Jorge Luis Borges and Enrique Anderson Imbert:

> En este aislamiento de invernadero o laboratorio con cristales hacia la realidad, pero sin contacto directo con ella, se han encerrado los jóvenes escritores que se llaman a sí mismos la *élite* de la generación actual. En ese aislamiento elaboran, con fragmentos de su propia realidad individual, de su ansiedad o de su histeria, un mundo de mágica realidad en el que las cosas cotidianas, iluminadas por un halo de alucinación y de angustia, se debaten en una lucha estéril por superar su pura materialidad. . . . El pecado mayor de estos escritores es haber perdido de vista la relación existente entre el poeta y la realidad, entre la literatura y la sociedad en que se produce, en haber querido hacer de la histeria privada la matriz del desorden público, haber elevado a la

categoría de héroes al impotente y al psicópata, haber sustituido la
auténtica rebelión con una estéril ansiedad y una angustia sin salida y
sin enemigos visibles.[6]

Thus forced to embrace such a diversity of literary styles and outlooks
the term is robbed of all critical value. The authors cited by Portuondo
as cultivators of magical realism have little in common except that
during the late 1940s they were not writing within the strict framework of socialist realism.

The wide currency of the term in contemporary Spanish-American literary criticism, however, derives from a paper entitled "Magical Realism in Spanish-American Fiction," which was read by Ángel
Flores at a meeting of the Modern Language Association of America
(New York, December 1954). The following year the text of Flores'
address was printed in *Hispania* and in 1957 a Spanish version
appeared in Mexico.[7] Unfortunately, the study by Flores suffers from
the same defect as that by Portuondo. Both critics take "magical
realism" as a blanket category to include all literature of psychological, philosophical or fantastic tendencies. Assuming that the
line of magical realists begins with Franz Kafka, Flores cites Jorge
Luis Borges (translator of Kafka into Spanish) as the originator of the
trend in Spanish America. And despite his inclusion of writers as
varied as Francisco Tario, Juan José Arreola, Eduardo Mallea, Enrique
Amorim, Adolfo Bioy Casares, Ernesto Sábato, Enrique Anderson
Imbert and a dozen others, he suggests that magical realism shows a
constant "preoccupation with style," "mathematical precision,"
"cold and cerebral and often erudite" writings that "approach that art
characterized by Ortega y Gasset as 'dehumanized.' "[8]

Here then we have the term "magical realism" applied to artistically refined and, in many cases, escapist literature—a usage quite
opposed to that intended by its originator Franz Roh, for whom
magical realism represented a means of access to the hidden mystery
of everyday reality. The word "magical" was chosen, he says, to
contrast with "mystical" or "supernatural" because "el misterio no
desciende al mundo representado, sino que se esconde y palpita tras
él."[9] Clearly there is an urgent need for some agreed-upon definition
if the term is to be of any use in literary criticism. In 1967 Luis Leal
undertook the task in an article differing with the position of Ángel
Flores and proposing a return to the original idea of Franz Roh.[10] Leal
marks out the boundaries of magical realism by indicating that it
cannot be identified with fantastic literature (no distortion of reality),
with surrealism (no oneiric motifs) or with psychological fiction (no
attempt to explain character motivation). But neither is it an aestheticist movement having a primary interest in stylistic refinement or

elaborate structures. Following Franz Roh, Leal states that magical realism is simply an attitude towards reality, an attitude in which the writer "se enfrenta a la realidad y trata de desentrañarla, de descubrir lo que hay de misterioso en las cosas, en la vida, en las acciones humanas."[11]

A child naturally views daily life in this way as something mysterious and magical, an open vision that the artist may recapture perhaps directly by evoking that circumscribed world lived only by the child. Such is the case of *El niño y el árbol* (1955), a short, lyrical novel by Antonio Souza that presents an intimate picture of a child's imagination. His universe centers around a cherry tree and is shared by a few people, as well as by animals, birds, insects, statues and pictures, all of which converse with the boy. Though well-conceived, the work is not uniformly successful or convincing; its structure is much too disjointed and the poetic tone is unevenly sustained. Imaginary friends, the familiar inventions of insecure children, figure prominently in "El duende" (1964) by Elena Garro and in "El gnomo" (1959) by Alberto Bonifaz Nuño. In the latter story, however, and in Juan Vicente Melo's "La noche alucinada" (1956), the magical world is in critical balance as the child, on the threshold of adolescence, is beginning to doubt its validity.

The Indian mind, like that of the child, mingles the real and the fantastic in a blend that must be accounted for in any literature that purports to treat the subject of the Indian with realism. Indeed, the magic, even the mythical view of reality is given central importance in the *indigenista* writings of Miguel Ángel Asturias:

> I will try to tell you, as simply as possible, what "magic realism" means to me. You see, an Indian or a mestizo in a small village might describe how he saw an enormous stone turn into a person or a giant or a cloud turn into a stone. That is not a tangible reality but one that involves an understanding of supernatural forces. That is why when I have to give it a literary label I call it "magic realism." But there are other similar kinds of occurrences. Due to an unfortunate accident, a woman falls into a chasm while going for water, or a rider is thrown from his horse. Such *affaires diverses*, as they could be called, can also be transformed into magic events. Suddenly, for the Indian or the mestizo, the woman didn't fall into the chasm, but the chasm grabbed her, simply because it needed a woman for a spring or for some other purpose. And the rider did not fall from his horse because he had a few drinks too many but because the stone on which he hit his head or the water in which he drowned called him. In this way stories grow into legends. The old Indian literature, the Indian books that were written before the Conquest of America by the Europeans, stories such as *Popul Vuh* or *Los anales de los Xahil* gain a kind of intermediate reality this way. Be-

tween the "real" and the "magic" there is a third sort of reality. It is a melting of the visible and the tangible, the hallucination and the dream. It is similar to what the surrealists around Breton wanted and it is what we could call "magic realism." "Magic realism," of course, has a direct relationship to the original mentality of the Indians. The Indian thinks in pictures; he sees things not so much as the events themselves but translates them into other dimensions, dimensions where reality disappears and dreams appear, where dreams transform themselves into tangible and visible forms.[12]

Thus tales of witchcraft and superstition are often recounted now as matters of fact, telling not of supernatural phenomena to arouse emotions in the reader, but of normal occurrences in a world where magic is inherent. "El anillo" (1964) by Elena Garro and "La piedra" (1964) by Rubén Marín are not open to logical or psychological explanation; they are simply true, however fantastic they may seem to the outsider. The little green men of "Cheneques" (1961) and the foul vapor that protects buried treasure in "Solimán" (1961) are not fanciful satires by their author Francisco González Pineda, but objective dramatizations of widely-held folk beliefs set in frank contrast with the modern world.

Nevertheless, the pure indigenous Indian population is rapidly disappearing, and it is the people of mixed ancestry who make up the majority of the populace in Mexico and most other Spanish-American republics. The extent to which Asturias himself writes of the mestizo and not just of the Indian can be judged from Ray Verzasconi's working definition of magical realism as he found it in this author's works. Magical realism, he concludes, is "an expression of the New World reality which at once combines the rational elements of the European super-civilization and the irrational elements of a primitive America."[13]

The continuing influence of the primitive past is forcefully depicted by Elena Garro in "La culpa es de los tlaxcaltecas" (1964), where an Indian warrior, the protagonist's husband in a previous existence, appears sporadically in her modern life. The woman keeps slipping from Mexico City today into another time dimension in which Tenochtitlán is the scene of a battle with the Spanish invaders. Finally, when her dual role becomes intolerable, she renounces the modern world and disappears with her Indian husband into the past that continues actual and indestructible. Superficially, Elena Garro's story resembles those fantastic tales of the eerie fourth dimension, but the annihilation of time here is not gratuitous or capricious. On the contrary, the work is a form of realism, since the nature of Mexican life is just such a marriage of the ancient with the modern.

Ten years earlier, in his first published work, *Los días enmascarados* (1954), Carlos Fuentes had shown a preoccupation with this theme of the inescapable pre-Hispanic past. Even the "masked days" of the title alludes to the mingling of pagan Indian beliefs with the Spanish or Christian ideals. The phrase, taken from the poem "El ídolo en el atrio" by José Juan Tablada, refers to five terrible *nemontemi* days at the end of the final year of the Aztec cycle:

> . . . .
> Y al final los días rezagados,
> Los Nemontemi . . . Cinco enmascarados
> Con pencas de maguey . . . .[14]
> . . . .

The best of the stories is "Chac Mool," in which an idol representing the Mayan and Toltec god of rain bought by Filiberto, the protagonist, in the Lagunilla market, comes to life and terrorizes him, finally to claim him as a sacrificial victim. "Por boca de los dioses" is a sort of companion piece, inasmuch as it treats the same theme. But, whereas "Chac Mool" simply relates what appears to be a supernatural event erupting in the world of palpable everyday reality, "Por boca de los dioses" is a hideous nightmare. As it begins, Oliverio is visiting an exhibition of modern painting in the Palacio de Bellas Artes with his friend Don Diego. The latter enjoys only the colonial works, but these Oliverio cannot tolerate. The men argue bitterly and Oliverio in anger cuts an Indian mouth from a painting by Tamayo and tries to take it away. They struggle and Don Diego falls through a high window to his death. When Oliverio returns to his hotel—the room number 1519 is an important figure in Mexico: the year of the invasion by Cortés— the mouth attacks him and fixes itself over his own, forcing him to speak in a way that is foreign to his nature. He tries to escape through the basement, but there he runs into the whole Aztec pantheon, including Tepoyollotl, Mayauel, Tezcatlipoca, Izpapalotl, Xolotl, Quetzalcóatl, Tecciztecatl and especially Tlazol, goddess of fertility, who pursues him relentlessly. He hides from her, but when she impugns his *machismo*, he has to present himself and is stabbed in the stomach. Filiberto and Oliverio are terrorized by the idol and the lips, and in the end both are taken in sacrifice—powerful symbols of the subordination of European culture to Mexico's indigenous heritage.

Similarly, in "Tlactocatzine, del jardín de Flandes" Fuentes's character is imprisoned forever by the ghost of an old woman whom we recognize from a series of clues, beginning with the title of the story (*tlactocatzine* is the Nahuatl word for "emperor"), as the aged and demented Carlota:

La luz blanca agitó mis cabellos, y la anciana me tomó de las manos, las besó; su piel apretó la mía. Lo supe por revelación, porque mis ojos decían lo que el tacto no corroboraba . . . y la voz, voz coagulada, eco de las sangres vertidas que aún transitan en cópula con la tierra. . . .

Esa noche escuché a mis espaldas—no sabía que lo iba a escuchar por siempre—el roce de las faldas sobre el piso; camina con una nueva alegría extraviada, sus ademanes son reiterativos y delatan satisfacción. Satisfacción de carcelero, de compañía, de prisión eterna. Satisfacción de soledades compartidas. Era su voz de nuevo, acercándose, sus labios junto a mi oreja, su aliento fabricado de espuma y tierra sepultada.[15]

Fuentes elaborates on this situation in his short novel *Aura* (1962), where the young history teacher, Felipe Montero, answers a classified newspaper advertisement by an old woman who wants an editor for the memoirs of her dead husband, General Llorente of Emperor Maximilian's forces. Felipe agrees to live in the same dark, airless apartment while doing the job, partly because he needs money and partly because of Aura, Madame Consuelo Llorente's attractive and mysterious niece. From the General's correspondence he learns that Consuelo must be 109 years old, and in a photograph he is astonished to see that the General's facial features are identical with his own. He falls in love with Aura, only to discover that she does not exist. In his arms he holds the old woman, who by force of will has been able to recover and project her own youth. The novel is pervaded by a strange oppressive atmosphere where dream is one with reality, the past with the present, and love with horror. The word *aura* itself is charged with this multiple and suggestive ambiguity: a gentle breeze, a breath, applause, general acceptance, epileptic or hysterical, and also a kind of vulture.

Outstanding among the experimental techniques employed by Fuentes is the conduct of the narration in the second person singular: "Lees ese anuncio . . . Lees y relees el aviso. Parece dirigido a ti, a nadie más. . . . Recoges tu portafolio . . ."[16] This device, probably inspired by Michel Butor's novel *La Modification* (1957), has the effect of drawing the reader into the story and making of him the protagonist; even the narrator becomes assimilated into the pro-tagonist as his consciousness.[17] Thus we see throughout the works of Carlos Fuentes a lasting preoccupation with the theme of social and political concepts that, though worn-out, anachronistic and re-pulsive, refuse to die and parasitically feed on the vitality of the present. Fuentes strives constantly to define the Mexican identity through his so-called "symbolic realism," the primary aim of which is, he says, to "percibir detrás de la apariencia fantasmagórica de las cosas una realidad más tangible, más maciza que la realidad evidente de todos los días."[18]

Cortés, Maximilian, and Carlota are but a few of the remarkable figures who have shaped the history of Mexico. And the other republics of the continent are similarly endowed with impressive national heroes, as Alejo Carpentier observed when visiting Haiti in 1943:

> A cada paso hallaba lo *real maravilloso*. Pero pensaba, además, que esa presencia y vigencia de lo real maravilloso no era privilegio único de Haití, sino patrimonio de la América entera, donde todavía no se ha terminado de establecer, por ejemplo, un recuento de cosmogonías. Lo real maravilloso se encuentra a cada paso en las vidas de hombres que inscribieron fechas en la historia del continente y dejaron apellidos aún llevados. . . .
>
> Y es que, por la virginidad del paisaje, por la formación, por la ontología, por la presencia fáustica del indio y del negro, por la revelación que constituyó su reciente descubrimiento, por los fecundos mestizajes que propició, América está muy lejos de haber agotado su caudal de mitologías. ¿Pero qué es la historia de América toda sino una crónica de lo real-maravilloso?[19]

It is not only America's history that possesses this marvelous or magical quality, but the nature of the physical geography of the continent, the terrain and climate of the interior, have effectively isolated large regions from the modern world. A person oppressed by his circumstances can actually escape into the past in Latin America where, traveling by air, one can easily reach stages of civilization equivalent to past ages—a theme which Carpentier himself elaborates in his superb novel, *Los pasos perdidos* (1953). In Mexican literature, however, there is an earlier work of remarkable similarity: *Sombra verde* (1949) by Ramiro Torres Septién. While the Mexican novel lacks Carpentier's sophistication, it is, nevertheless, an engrossing tale. Here the primitive, natural woman, who plays the same role as Rosario in *Los pasos perdidos* or Rima in W. H. Hudson's idealized *Green Mansions* (1904), is called Yaskara. As a character she is convincingly drawn, but obviously she also has a symbolic function, which her author has stated as follows:

> En mi novela, Yaskara es la fuga que los hombres ansiamos a menudo cuando la comunidad nos ahoga; es esa verdad innata que todos llevamos dentro; es ese principio animal y anárquico que nos provoca rebeldías contra normas, regímenes y costumbres que nos asfixian. Yaskara es la protesta contra la distorción que la humanidad hace de la vida del individuo.[20]

The magical conception of reality is not exclusive, however, to those nations with a population of indigenous or African descent. Just as the child perceives his world as enchanted, so the adult can strive for that exact focus which will reveal not the surface of reality but its essence. Such, for instance, is Ignacio Ibarra Mazari's story, "Una jaula en el balcón" (1963), about a kindly old woman who spends her time giving away sweets and conveying her greetings to everybody. One day she suddenly disappears; only her greetings remain, fluttering in the narrator's pocket until he buys a cage for them. Thus the most characteristic part of her personality is preserved. Paloma de Lille attempts the psycho-zoological type of literature associated with Rafael Arévalo Martínez, in which a person is identified closely with his totem animal. In her story "Sentada una gata estaba" (1963), the identification is complete. Slightly different is "Un nuevo procedimiento" (1946), by Francisco Rojas González, where noise is given the property of mass and a man commits suicide by sealing his room and turning on the radio. The accumulated noise of advertising and static crush him. Later, when the door is opened from outside, the sounds pour out all over the floor.

An effective technique for revealing the ineffable magic of reality is to suspend the normal flow of time. In the eternal moment sensations and perceptions are heightened for the lovers in Amparo Dávila's "Árboles petrificados" (1968). Still another means of drawing attention to the mystery of time is illustrated by Alfonso Reyes in "La Retro" (1953), where the protagonist suffers from a strange affliction following an automobile accident: he does everything in reverse —he walks backwards, takes dinner in the morning and breakfast at night, tells stories from the end to the beginning, and grows steadily shorter. Reyes's little experiment treating time like a magnetic tape or a motion picture operated in reverse antedates Alejo Carpentier's "Viaje a la semilla," although the latter more effectively raises the philosophical question of the actual validity of the concept of time.[21]

In "La hora inmóvil" (1962), Juan Vicente Melo gives a view of time that is perhaps more literary than real. This is a story of endless frustration, a single episode with no beginning and no end, destined to be repeated over and over. A mulatto named Crescencio has killed Gabriel Gálvez, taken his house and property and raped his daughter Maricel. Crescencio has two sons, one of them by Maricel; both are named Roberto. When Crescencio dies, Maricel's Roberto comes to the town to recover his grandfather's property, but the other Roberto, as if the unwilling agent of Destiny, kills him just as his father had killed old Gálvez. The narrator, the all-seeing eye, waits eagerly for the day when Roberto's son will arrive from the city to seek his vengeance. Roberto will always arrive, and the circumstances are fixed forever, static at this moment of revelation. The literary use of myth, in the sense of a "continuous parallel between contemporaneity and antiquity,"[22] reveals the mystery of the universal human situation—in this case, the archetypal mystery of the life cycle itself.

The town of Ixtepec in southern Mexico is both narrator and protagonist of Elena Garro's novel, *Los recuerdos del porvenir* (1963). Here too, history and time do not exist; the inhabitants of Ixtepec, now dead, have been and always will be victims of the eternal forces of tyranny and evil. In "La ciudad fantasma" (1959) Alberto Bonifaz Nuño recounts a young man's visit to one of those remote Mexican towns that survive somehow, the inhabitants living a ghostly existence sustained by illusions. They drive the city lad away out of fear because "el miedo que los vivos inspiran a los fantasmas, es todavía más agudo que el que los fantasmas inspiran a los vivos."[23] José Alvarado creates a poetically-charged atmosphere in *El personaje* (1955) around a man put off a train for want of a ticket in one of the abandoned towns so commonly found after the Revolution. As he wanders through the empty streets surrounded by visions and memories, the reader begins to wonder whether the man himself exists or if he merely serves to focus the reverberating illusions. The climate of this admirable novelette is similar to that of those famous ghost towns, Luvina and Comala, from the paralytic world of Juan Rulfo.

"Luvina" (1953) is a story without any plot or action. There is only the creation of an atmosphere of gloom, as a schoolmaster describes for a silent listener his stay in a dying, windswept mountain village named San Juan Luvina. He warns against ever going to this place where the few inhabitants are like phantoms rather than living human beings: "aquello es el purgatorio. Un lugar moribundo donde se han muerto hasta los perros y ya no hay ni quien le ladre al silencio; pues en cuanto uno se acostumbra al vendaval que allí sopla, no se oye sino el silencio que hay en todas las soledades."[24] The contrast with the world to which the teacher has now returned lends the magical quality to this vision and prefigures that other village of the dead: Comala.

In Comala, the setting of *Pedro Páramo* (1955), there is no clear line between death and life. The ghosts talk together from their graves and recall the past with nostalgia. The hellish portrait of Comala is relieved by memories of the Eden it once had been, until the wrath of the *cacique* Pedro Páramo brought about its destruction. Although Pedro Páramo himself hardly appears in the novel until the second half, he is of central importance to the whole, for, as Carlos Blanco Aguinaga has perceptively observed, "el cacique violento, por un lado, y por el otro, el amador abstraído, el soñador absorto, dramatiza en una sola figura poética el tipo contradictorio de existencia colectiva con que la nación mexicana se manifiesta en la historia."[25]

Rulfo writes in a simple, robust language that is based on popular speech, but elaborated and raised to the category of art. The structure

of his novel presents difficulties for the reader accustomed to a logically related sequence of events. In a procedure that is truer to life
than so-called photographic realism, the narrative is shattered into
fragments, in apparent disorder, from which the reader as coauthor
constructs an essential mosaic. Using such modern novelistic techniques and with a genius unequalled by any other writer, Juan Rulfo
has penetrated deeply into the marvelous quality of Mexican reality.

◇◇◇◇◇◇◇

The outstanding authors of magical realism in Mexico—Elena
Garro, Carlos Fuentes, and Juan Rulfo—employ once again many of
the motifs found in the folk-inspired tales of the supernatural. A
fundamental difference exists, however, in the attitude of the narrator
and in the resulting tone of magical realism. The uncanny phenomena of the supernatural tales revive old animistic beliefs and inspire
fear in the characters and uneasiness in the reader. The magical realist
may portray the same events, but in a matter-of-fact way, combining
reality with fantasy for a representation of the world that is not
uncanny but essentially true. The characters express no surprise at
shifts from one plane of reality to another, since the Indian and, to a
great extent, the *mestizo* already have a magical conception of the
world. We have seen how the surrealist also repeats elements from
folk tradition, not for their own sake but in personal visions that are
rooted in the reality of the unconscious mind. Surrealistic fiction in
which the *Doppelgänger* motif is employed, for instance, admits of a
possible explanation in the psychoneurotic dissociation of the
personality.

In contrast, no natural explanation is even appropriate for the
dual existence of the protagonist of Elena Garro's magical, yet realistic story "La culpa es de los tlaxcaltecas." She simply lives in
modern Mexico City and, simultaneously, in the Aztec capital Tenochtitlán. Both time and space are distorted by Garro in order to
reveal the continuing presence of Mexico's primitive past. Similarly,
Carlos Fuentes mixes indigenous elements with the modern to em-
phasize the actuality of the pre-Hispanic heritage, which he regards
as a sinister and inescapable impediment to social progress. In
"Luvina" Juan Rulfo carefully elaborates a realistic situation and then
progressively evokes the cold, oppressive atmosphere of his accursed
village, which diffuses into the original view of reality. The procedure is inverted in *Pedro Páramo*, where, from the beginning, the
reader is immersed in a static, airless world of heat and dust, in which
only the voices of the dead exist; gradually fragments of ghostly
conversation enable him to reconstruct an image of Comala when it

was alive. The stillness that results from the suspension of time in *Pedro Páramo* (and in the stories of Juan Vicente Melo, Amparo Dávila, Alberto Bonifaz Nuño, José Alvarado and Elena Garro) tends to accentuate the reality of the situation by eliminating sources of distraction and thus permitting the mind to enter fully into the experience. Further, it has the effect of removing the events described to the level of myth where they remain eternally true.

Born in a period of disillusionment, magical realism soon became an attitude of optimism and hope. Although the larger metaphysical questions perhaps will remain unanswered, this attempt is being made to find meaning after all in the small and simple aspects of life. A return to folk instincts and traditions helps to restore man's sense of wonder and has the purifying effect of renewing contact with basic human emotions. The magical realist, in order to apprehend the mysteries of reality, "exalta sus sentidos hasta un estado límite que le permite adivinar los inadvertidos matices del mundo externo, ese multiforme mundo en que vivimos."[26] Indeed, magical realism is peculiarly suited for capturing the essence of life in Latin America, where the complex European civilization is imperfectly blended with that of pagan indigenous peoples and where the ancient ways survive in the modern world.

Conclusion

The negligible attention that literature of fantasy and imagination receives from critics in Mexico is perhaps responsible for the mistaken general impression that very little is written there that is not regionalist in nature. The great majority of fantastic and imaginative Mexican literature is found, not surprisingly, expressed in short stories rather than longer narratives. The successful tale of the supernatural needs to be brief and intense in its creation of atmosphere, legends are normally related to single, specific episodes of history, and the novelty of a talking umbrella or cocoanut can not profitably be sustained for long. The visionary experience of hidden aspects of reality also must be recorded with strict unity of impression which extension could readily impair. In fact only forty-five novels were found, as compared with nearly seven hundred short stories. Predictably, almost half of the novels are utopias or science fiction, in which ample space is required for the depiction of entire new worlds.

Occasional fantasies appeared throughout the colonial period of Mexican history, but with the last decade of the nineteenth century came a surge of interest in spiritualism, in the exotic, and in aestheticism. This was the reaction of the *modernistas* to the new age of science and philosophical positivism. In the first years of the twentieth century, there was a notable decline in the amount of idealistic fiction published, but at no time did it disappear completely. During the turbulent years following the outbreak of the Mexican Revolution in 1910, members of the humanistic group known as the Ateneo de la

Juventud devoted their efforts to the spiritualization of the de-moralized country, and the *colonialista* writers sought meaning and order in a renewed exploration of the national past.

The fantastic narratives increased steadily in number until the end of the Second World War, when suddenly a flood of all classes of fantasy was produced. The coming of the Atomic Age had provoked mixed reactions in Mexico as elsewhere. Naturally, the conclusion of the war was cause for exultation and for new hopes for humanity, but, at the same time, the manner in which it had been brought to an end demonstrated that man would soon have the power to destroy all life on earth. Grave doubts about man's ability to use his new scientific knowledge wisely were reflected in Mexican literature by a ten-fold increase in the number of escapist fantasies and a three-fold increase in dire warnings cast as science fiction. From that time till the present, though never as an integrated movement, there has been a constant growth in the number of works produced in all categories of fantasy, except that concerning the miracles performed long ago by saintly priests.

Until the time of the Second World War, authors in Mexico generally made a simple choice between writing works of escapist fantasy and works of objective documentary realism. During the decade 1940–1950, however, another noteworthy feature was added to Mexican fiction. A new type of literature appeared which was not a form of escapism or aestheticism, but which was erroneously consid-ered to be fantasy since it failed to offer recognizable imitations of physical reality. Certain young writers led by Juan José Arreola and later by Carlos Fuentes were disregarding the powerful Spanish tradi-tion of regionalistic realism and were employing symbolic tech-niques to express other views of reality. The characteristic attitudes and techniques that formed these new works of imagination (not fantasy) were similar to those of the European Expressionist and Surrealist artists. Then, during the 1950s, a third type of imaginative literature appeared, casting on reality a peculiar, oblique focus: mag-ical realism. The volume of literature of the imagination now being published in Mexico year by year still does not approach that of objective realism, although it nearly equals that of the light, recre-ational literature of fantasy.

The extensive list of works of fantasy and imagination compiled in the present study does reveal that there are many works of dubious literary value, though perhaps not a higher proportion than would be found in realistic literature. But it also shows that many writers of ability have been attracted by these forms of literature. Among the authors who have cultivated fantasy we find Manuel Payno, Justo

Sierra, José María Roa Bárcena, Vicente Riva Palacio, Manuel Gutiérrez Nájera, Amado Nervo, José Vasconcelos, Francisco Monterde, Alfonso Reyes, Julio Torri, Gregorio López y Fuentes, José Rubén Romero, Francisco Rojas González, Francisco L. Urquizo, Martín Luis Guzmán, and Agustín Yáñez; and among the authors of literature of the imagination are Juan José Arreola, Juan Rulfo, Carlos Fuentes, Carlos Valdés, Elena Garro, Amparo Dávila, José Emilio Pacheco, and Salvador Elizondo. Despite the established reputations of these authors, literary critics and reviewers tend to regard their work of fantasy and imagination as aberrations to be dismissed out of hand merely because of the subject matter.

Literature as an art, however, does not depend simply on the ethical value of theme or subject matter, but also upon such aesthetic properties as unity, tone, style and structure. Undoubtedly, there is a place in literature for simple, ingenuous entertainments when they possess the beauty and charm of those by Alfonso Reyes and Julio Torri, or the audacity of those by Francisco Tario. The finely worked short stories of Reyes and Torri are pervaded by a subtle sense of humor that is rare in the Spanish American narrative. Reyes is invariably genial, lively and warm, whereas Torri is more biting and malicious, always dryly cynical. Both authors are great stylists of exceptional originality whose stories would reward closer critical attention than they have yet received. Francisco Tario also writes clear, refined prose, but the content of his inventions is completely unrestrained and extravagant. This arbitrary and ingenious author resolves the contradictions between reality and unreality and makes the most improbable situations convincing while he parodies the absurdities of life. The remarkable psychological penetration and compassion with which his characters are drawn demonstrate that fantasy fiction can indeed have human and moral validity, despite the idealistic philosophy on which it is founded. The works of Francisco Tario constitute the most outstanding contribution to literature of fantasy in Mexico.

During the course of this study it has been observed that themes of social importance are often effectively expressed by means of intuition and symbolic techniques, more effectively perhaps than would be possible with straightforward descriptive realism. Among the most noteworthy of the authors who consider logic and objective transcription to be incapable of apprehending certain aspects of reality are Juan José Arreola, Salvador Elizondo, and Amparo Dávila. Arreola's concise, ironic parables and satires that aspire to formal perfection follow in the tradition of Reyes and Torri. He is motivated, though, by a more serious concern with philosophical and social questions. Handling a limited number of themes—the impossibility of love between man and woman, the depreciation of moral values and the failure of the Church, existential solitude, and death—Arreola has set down an intensely personal vision of reality. Similarly, Amparo Dávila and Salvador Elizondo have provided insights into the unconscious psychic life of man. Their tormented characters inhabit a world that defies rational explanation, but which conveys to the reader a powerful sense of alienation and spiritual anguish.

The works of Carlos Fuentes and Juan Rulfo are characterized by a continuing endeavour to define the nature of Mexican reality. These two authors have employed to good advantage that special focus or attitude which is known as "magical realism" and which seeks to reveal the hidden, mysterious qualities that underlie daily life. Fuentes is especially preoccupied with the theme of the undying influence of Mexico's pre-Hispanic past which saps the vitality of the present, a theme that he develops by means of simultaneous, intermingled planes of reality, both ancient and modern. Juan Rulfo, on the other hand, envisions an eternal, airless world of rancor, violence and death in his search for the soul of Mexico. This highly poeticized vision is admirably suited to the author's purpose, for he has derived it (and the language with which he expresses it) from the people themselves. Magical realism, particularly of the type created by Fuentes and Rulfo— abstracting myth from reality—is a new and important contribution to the prose fiction of Spanish America.

Literature of the imagination has enabled Mexican prose fiction to break free from the limitations of regionalism, to penetrate to the essential qualities of reality by treating the narrative as art rather than document. Both fantasy and the most ambitious literature of the imagination are founded on the traditional elements of folklore. For these motifs which spring out of deep-seated popular beliefs, each author finds a special significance and function. But in whatever way the materials of folk tradition are employed in literature and for whatever purpose—whether to tell a story for entertainment or as a way to metaphysical knowledge, to give aesthetic pleasure or to teach a lesson—its effect is to prompt the reader to reflect on the complexities of human existence.

Notes to Chapters

NOTES TO THE PREFACE

1. The common view of Mexican fiction is illustrated in the following series of critical statements: Carleton Beals concludes a survey of the Mexican novel from Lizardi to Azuela with the observation that "in any case, the Mexican novel has established a tradition in the realm of realism" (*Mexican Maze* [Philadelphia and London: J. P. Lippincott, 1931], p. 276); in the novel of the 1930s and 1940s, the novel of the continuing Mexican Revolution, Adalbert Dessau identifies one constant feature: "El requisito indispensable consiste en que los autores se vuelvan hacia los hombres de pueblo, hacia temas relacionados con los problemas nacionales, y que creen una forma de narrativa popular que satisfaga las necesidades del público, especialmente en obras de realismo crítico. . . . Los escritores revolucionarios más representativos conocían las corrientes modernas—en su época—de la literatura universal. . . . Al conocimiento del desarrollo de la literatura internacional debieron ciertos impulsos para su obra. Pero lo principal es su confrontación con la realidad y la tradición literaria de su propio pueblo" (*La novela de la Revolución mexicana*, trans. Juan José Utrilla [México: Fondo de Cultura Económica, 1972], pp. 469–471); Manuel Pedro González says categorically that "la novela fantástica es un género que cuenta con muy pocos y muy mediocres adeptos en Hispanoamérica. En México son contados los que actualmente la frecuentan" (*Trayectoria de la novela en México* [México: Ediciones Botas, 1951], p. 410); Genaro Fernández Mac Gregor characterizes the typical short story of the 1950s as "para mi modo de ver las cosas, demasiado crudo; tiende a un realismo brutal, de mal gusto" (in an interview with Emmanuel Carballo, *19 protagonistas de la literatura mexicana del siglo XX* [México: Empresas Editoriales, 1965], p. 58); Agustín Yáñez, interviewed early in the 1960s, describes "la novelística de hoy día" as "un movimiento en ebullición en el que se pueden señalar ciertos rasgos característicos. . . . Uno de ellos consiste en enfocar la novela hacia los grandes problemas de la vida nacional, con sentido realista y crítico." Mexican novelists today cultivate, he says, "lo que yo llamo el 'retrato crítico'. . . . El retratar a la realidad con el fin de descubrir sus fallas e intentar el diseño de su posible superación" (in Emmanuel Carballo, *19 protagonistas* . . ., pp. 303–304); and finally José Luis Martínez, who in 1949 observed that "la mayoría de los novelistas mexicanos de las últimas décadas se han entregado a la descripción de lo bajo, lo miserable y lo horrible, animados por una plausible conciencia de justicia social, aunque poco atentos a los fines y a la eficacia de sus obras. Los afirma en su decisión el sentir que prosiguen una robusta tradición mexicana" (*Literatura mexicana siglo XX: 1910–1949* [México: Antigua Librería Robredo, 1949], I, 258), a decade later, on the occasion of his admission to the Academia Mexicana, declares that the tradition remains unchanged: "las características más constantes de la prosa mexicana . . . hecha de vivacidad y de sentido directo, movida como por una urgencia interior y elaborada con incipiente retórica, y cuyo mérito, por todo ello, no reside tanto en su calidad intrínseca sino en el peso y la emoción de su mensaje;. . . . Movidos por corrientes culturales y por cierta idiosincracia mexicana, nuestros escritores han preferido los dominios de lo sentimental, las luchas y los conflictos ideológicos y los problemas sociales inmediatos, y han dejado a un lado los análisis morales de la conducta y la convivencia humanas, la reflexión filosofía y la imaginación" (*De la naturaleza y carácter de la literatura mexicana* [México: Fondo de Cultura Económica, 1960], pp. 51–52, 54).

2. *Webster's New World Dictionary,* College Edition (Toronto, 1953).

3. *Webster's New Collegiate Dictionary* (Springfield, Mass., 1956).

4. The reader interested in children's literature in Mexico is referred to the following studies by Blanca Lydia Trejo: *La literatura infantil en México desde los aztecas hasta nuestros días: información, crítica, orientación* (México: n.p., 1950); "La literatura infantil," *El libro y el pueblo,* 16, No. 2 (feb. 1954), 5–22; "La narración del cuento infantil," *El libro y el pueblo,* 17, No. 19 (sept.–oct. 1955), 76–80.

NOTES TO CHAPTER I

1. *The Standard Edition of the Complete Psychological Works of Sigmund Freud,* ed. James Strachey, trans. Alix Strachey, XVII (London: The Hogarth Press and the Institute of Psycho-analysis, 1955), pp. 247–248.

2. "Cartas americanas," in *Obras completas,* 2a ed. (Madrid: M. Aguilar, 1947), III, 293.

3. This feature of Vasconcelos' thought bears a clear relationship to Arthur Schopenhauer's theory of music as the purest expression of will, the universal language capable of revealing the inmost essence of things:

> We can regard the phenomenal world, or nature, and music as two different expressions of the same thing; and this thing itself is therefore the only medium of their analogy, a knowledge of which is required if we are to understand that analogy. Accordingly, music, if regarded as an expression of the world, is in the highest degree a universal language that is related to the universality of concepts much as these are related to the particular things. . . . All possible efforts, stirrings, and manifestations of the will, all the events that occur within man himself and are included by the reasoning faculty in the wide, negative concept of feeling, can be expressed by the infinite number of possible melodies, but always in the universality of mere form without the material, always only according to the in-itself, not to the phenomenon, as it were the innermost soul of the phenomenon without the body. This close relation that music has to the true nature of all things can also explain the fact that, when music suitable to any scene, action, event, or environment is played, it seems to disclose to us its most secret meaning, and appears to be the most accurate and distinct commentary on it. Moreover, to the man who gives himself up entirely to the impression of a symphony, it is as if he saw all the possible events of life and of the world passing by within himself. Yet if he reflects, he cannot assert any likeness between that piece of music and the things that passed through his mind. For, as we have said, music differs from all the other arts by the fact that it is not a copy of the phenomenon, or, more exactly, of the will's adequate objectivity, but is directly a copy of the will itself, and therefore expresses the metaphysical to everything physical in the world, the thing-in-itself to every phenomenon. (Arthur Schopenhauer, *The World as Will and Representation,* trans. E. F. J. Payne [New York: Dover, 1958], I, 262.)

Vasconcelos no doubt is aware of his indebtedness to Schopenhauer. In his *Manual de filosofía* (México: Botas, 1940) he observes:

En estética dejó Schopenhauer una veta rica, cuando distinguió el valor de la música. Su tesis sobre la belleza del panorama y la plástica es platónica; es bello, según él, lo individual que representa, sugiere, lo universal. En sus profundas divagaciones sobre la música llega a una conclusión trascendental cuando declara: "que la música no es como las otras artes una copia de las ideas, sino representación de la voluntad misma." La música nos muestra la eterna, bregadora, aventurera voluntad, volviendo sobre sí misma, para volver a empezar. La música al remover nuestras emociones, se dirige a algo más sutil que el intelecto; las demás artes hablan de cosas y de sombras, la música habla de la cosa en sí kantiana. El concepto estético comienza a libertarse, de esta suerte, del intelectualismo que le ha impedido definirse según su propia naturaleza. (José Vasconcelos, *Obras completas* [México: Libreros Mexicanos Unidos, 1961], IV, 1142.)

4. "La casa imantada," *La sonata mágica: cuentos y relatos,* 2a ed. (Buenos Aires and México: Espasa-Calpe Argentina, 1950), pp. 28–29.

5. "Alma de agua," *Cuentos mayas y fantasías* (México: Editora Ibero-Mexicana, 1955), p. 23.

6. For a discussion of comparable beliefs found in New Caledonia, New Guinea, Central and South Africa, Greece, and India relating mirrors to the human soul, see Sir James G. Frazer, *The Golden Bough: A Study in Magic and Religion,* abridged ed. (New York: Macmillan, 1951), pp. 222–223.

7. "La polka de los Curitas," *Tapioca Inn: mansión para fantasmas* (México: Tezontle, 1952), p. 27.

8. "Holes in Nothing," *Mr. Tomkins Explores the Atom* (New York: Macmillan, 1944), pp. 77–86.

9. "El arma secreta," *Todos los cuentos de Rafael Solana* (México: Ediciones Oasis, 1961), p. 164.

10. *El laberinto de la soledad,* 7a ed. (México: Fondo de Cultura Económica, 1969), pp. 52–53.

11. "La vida del campo," *Tres libros* (México: Fondo de Cultura Económica, 1964), p. 17.

12. "El fusilado," *La sonata mágica: cuentos y relatos,* 2a. ed. (Buenos Aires and México: Espasa-Calpe Argentina, 1950), p. 22.

13. Ibid., p. 23.

14. Melo outlined his brief autobiography in a talk in the Instituto Nacional de Bellas Artes on September 9, 1965, which was published later in *Los narradores ante el público* (México: Joaquín Mortiz, 1966), pp. 167–176. He gives more details in *Juan Vicente Melo* (México: Empresas Editoriales, 1966), a small volume published in Emmanuel Carballo's admirable series *Nuevos Escritores Mexicanos del Siglo XX Presentados Por Sí Mismos.*

15. In 1954 the Universidad Nacional Autónoma de México published the second edition of Juan de la Cabada's stories *Paseo de mentiras*. A filmed version of "María 'La voz' " was directed in the same year by Julio Bracho.

16. *L 'Érotisme* (Paris: Les Editions de Minuit, 1957), p. 25.

17. The identification of fear as a source of the sublime was made in the eighteenth century by Edmund Burke and expressed in his theoretical study

A Philosophical Enquiry into the Origin of our Ideas of the Sublime and Beautiful [1766]. A recent edition has been prepared by J. T. Boulton and published by Routledge and Paul (London, 1958).

18. Charles Baudelaire, "Danse macabre," *Les Fleurs du mal* [1857] in his *Oeuvres complètes*, ed. Yves Florenne (Paris: Le Club Français du Livre, 1966), I, 965.

19. *The Supernatural in Fiction* (London: Peter Nevill, 1952), p. 11.

20. "El éxodo," *Una violeta de más: cuentos fantásticos* (México: Editorial Joaquín Mortiz, 1968), p. 99.

21. "La banca vacía," *Una violeta de más*, p. 182.

22. *Art and Society* (London: Heinemann, 1937), p. 268.

NOTES TO CHAPTER II

1. Lord Raglan, "Myth and Ritual," *Journal of American Folklore*, 270 (Oct.–Dec. 1955), 461.

2. Francisco Monterde, *Literatura universal*, 3a ed. (México: Secretaría de Educación Pública, 1963), p. 25.

3. Vicente Riva Palacio, "La leyenda de un santo," *Cuentos del General* (México: Editora Nacional, 1963), p. 100.

4. Ibid., p. 101.

5. Idem.

6. *The Century after Cortés*, trans. Joan MacLean (Chicago: University of Chicago Press, 1965), pp. 106–107.

7. Carlos Samayoa Chinchilla gives another version of this legend, with Guatemala as the setting: "La lagartija de esmeraldas," *La casa de la muerta: cuentos y leyendas de Guatemala* (Guatemala, 1941).

8. A lyrical dramatization of the legend by Carmen Toscano—in one act, and including music and ritual dances—was performed in the open air at Plaza de Chimalístac, Mexico City, in 1958. The text was published subsequently· by the Fondo de Cultura Económica in its Colección Tezontle (México, 1959).

9. *Historia de las cosas de Nueva España*, ed. Angel María Garibay K., 2a ed. (México: Editorial Porrúa, 1969), I, 46 [Bk. 1, chap. 6].

10. Ibid., IV, 24 [Bk. 12, chap. 1].

11. "Wailing Women of Folklore," *Journal of American Folklore*, 82, No. 325 (Jul.–Sept. 1969), 270–272.

12. Luis Leal cites "La Calle de don Juan Manuel" (1835) by José Justo Gómez de la Cortina as "el primer cuento legendario de que tenemos noticia" (*Breve historia del cuento mexicano* [México, 1956], p. 34), an assertion that presumably depends on his definition of the term "cuento." In fact, Carlos Sigüenza y Góngora's earlier *Paraíso occidental* was not primarily a work of narrative impulse but the commissioned history of a particular convent.

13. *A Plain and Literal Translation of the Arabian Nights' Entertainments, Now Entitled the Book of the Thousand Nights and a Night . . .* by Richard F. Burton (London: Printed by the Burton Club for Private Subscribers Only, 1885), p. 290.

14. "Leyenda de la Tatuana," *Leyendas de Guatemala* (Madrid: Ediciones Oriente, 1930).

15. "El barco de la Tatuana," *Han de estar y estarán* (Santiago, Chile: Editorial Zig-Zag, 1938).

16. Vicente Riva Palacio and Juan de Dios Peza, "La leyenda de la Calle de Olmedo," *Tradiciones y leyendas mexicanas* (México, 1900).

17. "La Calle de Olmedo. Ahora 6a. del Correo Mayor," *Las calles de México: leyendas y sucedidos* (México: Ediciones León Sánchez, 1922), pp. 159–166.

18. Nancy Moore, "Legend," *Dictionary of World Literature*, ed. Joseph T. Shipley; rev. ed. (New York: Philosophical Library, 1953), p. 249.

19. "Papeles sobre las letras: la literatura fantástica," *Los domingos del profesor: ensayos* (México: Editorial Cvltvra, 1965), p. 23.

20. "Las rosas de Juan Diego," *Cuentos y poemas* (México: UNAM, 1964), p. 29.

21. Ibid., p. 30.

22. The quotation is from the satirical novel by Anatole France, *L'Île des pingouins* (orig. 1908), Book II, Chapter V.

23. "El Señor Aquél," *Nivel*, No. 2 (feb. 25, 1959), 6.

24. Idem.

25. Idem.

26. See note 19 above.

27. "El 'ángel caído,'" in his *Cuentos misteriosos*, ed. Alfonso Reyes (Madrid: Biblioteca Nueva, 1921), XX, 87.

28. This motif had previously been employed by the Portuguese novelist Eça de Queiroz in one of his letters from *A Correspondência de Fradique Mendes* (1891), usually known as "Um homem de talento"; and also by the Venezuelan Pedro Emilio Coll in "El diente roto" (*El paso errante*, 1948). In these versions, the protagonist maintains absolute silence and lets others suppose he is reflecting upon important matters. Invariably, he is awarded high public office.

29. *El Padre Eterno, Satanás y Juanito García* (México: Editorial Botas, 1938), p. 104.

30. "Un viaje al Cielo" in *Cuentos mexicanos* (México: Tip. de "El Nacional", 1898), p. 75.

31. *Latin America: A General History*, 2nd ed. (New York: Macmillan, 1969), p. 522.

32. *The Devil in Legend and Literature* (Chicago: Open Court, 1931), p. 274.

33. [Juan F.] Vereo Guzmán, *La rebelión de Satán: novela fantástica con final probable dedicada a Nuestra Señora de la Ironía* (México: Ediciones Populares "Atalaya" [1945?]), p. 33.

34. V[icente] García de Diego, ed., *Antología de leyendas de la literatura universal* (Madrid: Editorial Labor, 1953), p. 3.

NOTES TO CHAPTER III

1. The strong tradition of critical realism in Mexican fiction has already been described. (See "Preface," Note No. 1.) During the last twenty years the achievements of such writers as Juan José Arreola, Juan Rulfo and Carlos Fuentes have led to a reluctant acknowledgement that the nature of the Mexican narrative may be changing. But recognition need not imply approval. Prose fiction in Mexico has generally been accepted as a vehicle for social criticism; any deviation from this attitude is regarded with suspicion: for Ermilo Abreu Gómez "la novela mexicana . . . ha de salir al mundo nuevo de la vida creada por nuestras conmociones sociales" ("Novela premiada: Francisco Rojas González, *La negra Angustias*," *Letras de México*, 6, No. 1 [enero 1945], 5), and "tiene que descansar en el conflicto de explotados y explotadores, sin hablar de criollos e indios" (quoted by Juan Miguel de Mora V., "Panorama de la novela en México; 6a parte," *Hoy* [jul. 20, 1946], p. 48); the short stories by Carlos Fuentes are accused of "cierta ferocidad subjetiva, un alambicado afán de *incomunicación* claramente emparentados con la sensibilidad privativa de los círculos literarios 'elegantes.' . . . una seudo-aristocracia intelectual, tradicionalmente insulsa y anodina." They are seen as representing "un neoacademismo estéril y desafecto a cualquier contacto fecundador" and not that praiseworthy "literatura que se rebela de modo auténtico contra la injusticia. . . . La que no sacrifica la ética en aras de una belleza 'pura' imposible" (Joaquín Macgregor, "En torno a un folleto," *Revista mexicana de cultura*, No. 403 [dic. 19, 1954], 12); although fantasy "no tiene justificación, sí tiene explicación . . . su razón histórica . . . ha surgido en los momentos en que la intelligenzia burguesa ya no puede darse el lujo de mirar de frente a la realidad, porque la realidad sólo puede revelarse que sus días están contados. . . . La 'literatura fantástica' de nuestros días es la literatura de avestruz" (José Luis González, "Cuatro cuestiones," in *México en la cultura*," No. 336 [agosto 28, 1955], 3); it is "literatura evasiva y, por tanto, nada americana, aunque bastante elogiada por sus amigos. El autor [Carlos Fuentes] no da un paso si no pone sus ojos en la decrépita literatura inglesa" (Alfredo Hurtado, "Los Presentes," *Estaciones*, 1, No. 3 [otoño, 1956], 396); both un-Mexican and exhibitionist "Tanto la novela fantástica como los cuentos de hadas son expresiones autóctonas, tan congénitas y naturales en el ambiente físico, en la tradición y el espíritu de aquellas literaturas nórdicas como su flora y su fauna. En la América nuestra, en cambio, resultan artificiosos, intelectualizados y contrahechos. . . . En nuestras novelas fantásticas, más que el genio creador, priva el ingenio, y una actitud frívola y como de juego. Dan la impresión de mero deporte intelectual, de regodeo vanidoso y superficial. Casi todos estos autores están más interesados en lucirse, en exhibir los artilugios de su fantasía y las habilidades y recursos de su ingenio que en crear obra de monto y noble poesía. Todos escriben para

lucir su virtuosismo mental ante una élite muy reducida y gustadora de estos manjares exóticos. En América, esta expresión resulta artificial, artificiosa y sofisticada—sobre todo sofisticada. Pero a base de pura sofistiquería jamás se ha producido obra de tamaño mayor en ninguna lengua. Es literatura para minorías ociosas, frívolas y snob, literatura exhibicionista" (Manuel Pedro González, "Leopoldo Marechal y la novela fantástica," *Cuadernos americanos*, 151 [1967], 203–204); in the opinion of José Vasconcelos "la literatura debe ser, fundamentalmente, protesta. Su raíz es la libertad" (in an interview with Emmanuel Carballo, *19 protagonistas de la literatura mexicana del siglo XX* [México: Empresas Editoriales, 1965], p. 21); equally categorical is Antonio Magaña Esquivel, according to whom "la literatura es, esencialmente, la conciencia de un pueblo; no se le puede apartar de las condiciones sociales, ni de su función social, ni de su compromiso en lo más hondo de la lucha" (*La novela de la Revolución* [México: Instituto Nacional de Estudios Históricos de la Revolución Mexicana, 1964], I, 11).

2. *La originalidad de Rubén Darío* (Buenos Aires: Centro Editor de América Latina, 1967), p. 216.

3. "El descontento y la promesa," *Seis ensayos en busca de nuestra expresión* (Buenos Aires, 1926.) In his *Obra crítica,* ed. E. S. Speratti Piñero (México: Fondo de Cultura Económica, 1960), p. 253. The essay was originally delivered in Buenos Aires as a lecture to the Asociación Amigos del Arte on Aug. 28, 1926 and was printed the following day in the newspaper *La Nación.*

4. "La literatura maravillosa," in *Obras completas,* ed. Francisco González Guerrero and Alfonso Méndez Plancarte, 3a ed. (Madrid: Aguilar, 1962), II, 706.

5. "The Poetic Principle," *Complete Works of Edgar Allan Poe* (New York: Fred De Fau and Co., 1902), I, 171. "The Poetic Principle" was Poe's last lecture, delivered shortly before his death in 1849. The text was published posthumously in *Sartain's Union Magazine* (Oct. 1850).

6. Henri Aime Casavant reports that the story was used without permission in the successful 1942 film *Tales of Manhattan,* directed by Julien Duvivier for Twentieth Century Fox Studios. Rojas González complained, but the coproducer on whom the blame was cast proved to be insolvent. In any case, the author had neglected to register the copyright for his story and received no compensation. See Casavant's master's thesis "Francisco Rojas González, cuentista"·(México: UNAM, 1962), p. 15.

7. Quoted by Elena Poniatowska in "Siluetas del periodismo mexicano: José Alvarado escritor político," *Revista de la Universidad de México*, 13, No. 5 (1959), 14.

8. Nervo, *Obras*, I, 253.

9. Destiny is given material form by Amado Nervo in "El obstáculo" (1921); virtue, by Carlos Villamil Castillo in "El expendio de virtudes" (1949); revenge, by Manuel Becerra Acosta in "El vendedor de venganzas" (1945); pain, by Manuel Romero de Terreros in "La tumba desconocida" (1909); and sorrow, by Jorge Useta in "La muerte de la pena" (1932).

10. It should be noted that Alfonso Reyes created this autonomous character one year before Unamuno published *Niebla* (1914) and eight years

before the production of Pirandello's epoch-making *Sei personaggi in cerca d'autore* (1921). Further examples of the autonomous character in Mexican fiction are Xavier Icaza's bizarre *estridentista* novel, *Panchito Chapopote* (1928); "Personajes de personajes o complicaciones pirandelianas" (1932) by Jorge Useta [José Ugarte]; and "Escaramuza" (1961) by Lourdes Garza Quesada.

11. "Diálogo de Aquiles y Helena," *Verdad y mentira* (Madrid: Aguilar, 1950), p. 89.

12. "Sila," *Revista de la Universidad de México*, 17, No. 8 (1962), 14.

13. Ibid., p. 16.

14. The director of the film was Juan Guerrero and the featured actors were Enrique Álvarez Félix, Héctor Bonilla, and Amedée Chabot. An unfavorable review by Jorge Ayala Blanco appeared in *La cultura en México*, No. 424 [Supplement of *Siempre!*, No. 874], (marzo 25, 1970), p. xv.

15. *El Dr. Fu Chang Li* (México: Pablo y Henrique González-Casanova, 1945), p. 11.

16. Ibid., p. 18.

17. Ibid., p. 24.

18. Borges in *El escritor y su obra: entrevistas de Georges Charbonnier con Jorge Luis Borges* (México: Siglo XXI Editores, 1967), pp. 10–11.

19. Jean-Paul Sartre as quoted by René Huyghe, *Art and the Spirit of Man*, trans. Norbert Guterman (New York: Harry N. Abrams, 1962), p. 476.

20. Josef Von Sternberg's classic film *The Blue Angel* (1929), starring Emil Jannings and Marlene Dietrich, was based on the novel *Professor Unrat oder das Ende eines Tyrannen* (Munich, 1905–1906) by Heinrich Mann.

21. Elizondo's story derives ultimately from "The Infinite Dream of Pao-Yü," a chapter of the *Hung Lou Meng* or *Dream of the Red Chamber* (1792) by Ts'ao Hsueh-ch'in. In this eighteenth-century Chinese novel, Pao-Yü dreams that he is in a garden just like his own when two young ladies of his acquaintance speak to him, but then apologize for having mistaken him for Pao-Yü. He then climbs over a wall and enters another garden which is his own. In the house he can see Pao-Yü sleeping. As he watches, the young ladies awaken Pao-Yü and ask what he dreamt. He tells them that he dreamt he was in a garden, that the girls did not recognize him and that he found Pao-Yü sleeping in his bed. On hearing this from outside the room, Pao-Yü enters saying that he is looking for a Pao-Yü. The Pao-Yü in bed greets him but just then a voice from outside calls "Pao-Yü!" The dream Pao-Yü leaves. Pao-Yü wakes up and the ladies ask what he dreamt. He replies that he had a strange dream that he was in a garden. . . . This story was given wide circulation in Spanish America when Borges included it in *Antología de la literatura fantástica*, eds. J. L. Borges, S. Ocampo, and A. Bioy Casares (Buenos Aires: Editorial Sudamericana, 1940), pp. 276–277. Lewis Carroll introduced the idea into English fiction in *Through the Looking-Glass and What Alice Found There* (1896):

> "It's only the Red King snoring. . . . He's dreaming now," said Tweedledee: "and what do you think he's dreaming about?"
> Alice said "Nobody can guess that."

"Why, about *you!*" Tweedledee exclaimed, clapping his hands triumphantly. "And if he left off dreaming about you, where do you suppose you'd be?"

"Where I am now, of course," said Alice.

"Not you!" Tweedledee retorted contemptuously. You'd be nowhere. Why, you're only a sort of thing in his dream!"

"If that there King was to wake," added Tweedledum, "you'd go out—bang!—just like a candle!"

(*Alice in Wonderland and Other Favorites* [New York: Pocket Books, 1951], pp. 166–167.)

Undoubtedly, Elizondo is familiar with Borges's adaptation of the concept in "Las ruinas circulares" (*Sur*, No. 75 [1940], 100–106).

22. Probably the most important early review of Borges's work published in Mexico was by Xavier Villaurrutia: "Sobre *Ficciones*," *El hijo pródigo*, 8, No. 26 (1945), 119.

23. Prominent among the young disciples of Borges in Mexico were José Emilio Pacheco, Raymundo Ramos Gómez, Florencio Sánchez Cámara, and Salvador Elizondo.

NOTES TO CHAPTER IV

1. *El réferi cuenta nueve* (México: Editorial Cvltvra, 1943), pp. 62–63.

2. Ibid., p. 154.

3. For an account of Rivas's trial by the Holy Inquisition see Pablo González Casanova, *La literatura perseguida en la crisis de la Colonia* (México: El Colegio de México, 1958), pp. 106–110.

4. *Utopias in Literature since the Romantic Period* (Christchurch, New Zealand: University of Canterbury, 1968), pp. 50–51.

5. *New Maps of Hell* (London: The New English Library, 1963), p. 17.

6. Ibid., p. 14.

7. Quoted by William Whitehead, "The Science of Science Fiction," C.B.C. radio program, Dec. 16, 1965.

8. Recent appearances of such monsters in Mexican space fantasy are "Los hemoglobitas" (1966) by Alfredo Cardona Peña, and "El error" (1967) by J. J. Fábregas.

9. Prologue to *Un hombre más allá del universo* (México: Botas, 1935), p. 5.

10. Amis, *New Maps of Hell*, p. 74.

11. *Los domadores y otras narraciones*, 2a ed. (México: Libro-Mex Editores, 1960), pp. 22–23.

12. Human bodies may now be frozen (cryonic suspension) by arrangement with the Cryonic Society of New York. After the body is installed in a capsule (costing $3,000) filled with liquid nitrogen, the Society will (for a minimum fee of $10,000) care for it until such time as medical science is able

to revive and rejuvenate it. As yet, the law denies this service to living persons who believe that cures for their specific diseases will eventually be discovered.

13. *Cuentos de magia, de misterio y de horror* (México: Finisterre, 1966), p. 118.

14. *Tiene la noche un árbol* (México: Fondo de Cultura Económica, 1958), p. 96.

NOTES TO CHAPTER V

1. *An Experiment in Criticism* (Cambridge: Cambridge University Press, 1961), p. 50.

2. Samuel Taylor Coleridge, *Biographia Literaria*, ed. John Shawcross (Oxford: Oxford University Press, 1907), I, 202.

3. "Imagination," *Webster's New Collegiate Dictionary*, 2nd ed. (Springfield, Mass.: G. and C. Merriam, 1956).

4. Sigmund Freud as quoted by Lionel Trilling in "Freud and Literature," *The Liberal Imagination* (Garden City, N.Y.: Doubleday, 1953), p. 44.

5. *Vida de Hoffmann*, trans. Teba Bronstein (Buenos Aires: Editorial Argonauta, 1945), p. 191.

6. Dorothy L. Sayers, Introd. to *Great Short Stories of Detection, Mystery and Horror* (London: Gollancz, 1928), p. 45.

7. In *Los narradores ante el público* (México: Editorial Joaquín Mortiz, 1966), p. 133.

8. "Música concreta," *Música concreta* (México: Fondo de Cultura Económica, 1964), p. 36.

9. Ibid., p. 18.

10. Quoted by Herbert Read, *Art and Society* (London: William Heinemann, 1937), p. 253.

11. Quoted by Jacques Hardré, "Surrealism," *Encyclopedia of Poetry and Poetics*, ed. Alex Preminger (Princeton, N.J.: Princeton University Press, 1965), p. 821.

12. "El jardín de las tumbas," *Música concreta* (México: Fondo de Cultura Económica, 1964), p. 56.

13. Aurora M. Ocampo de Gómez, in *Diccionario de escritores mexicanos*, ed. A. M. Ocampo de Gómez and Ernesto Prado Velázquez (México: Universidad Nacional Autónoma de México, 1967), p. 94.

14. "La Démystification par l'humour noir," *L'Avant scène* (fev. 15, 1959). Quoted by Martin Esslin, *The Theatre of the Absurd* (Garden City, N.Y.: Doubleday, 1961), p. 133.

15. "El epitalamio de Onésimo Segundo," *El dominó* (México: Pájaro Cascabel, 1964), p. 56.

16. "La noche de los genios raros," *La noche del féretro y otros cuentos de la noche* (México: Editorial Novaro-México, 1958), pp. 117–118.

17. C. G. Jung, "Psychology and Literature," in his *Modern Man in Search of a Soul*, trans. W. D. Dell and C. F. Baynes [orig. 1933] (New York: Harcourt, Brace and World, 1970), p. 158.

NOTES TO CHAPTER VI

1. *Art and Society* (London: William Heinemann, 1937), p. 252.

2. Arturo B. Fallico, *Art and Existentialism* (Englewood Cliffs, N.J.: Prentice-Hall, 1962), pp. 129–130.

3. José Luis González, "Cuatro cuestiones," *México en la cultura*, No. 336 [Suppl. *Novedades*] (Agosto 28, 1955), p. 3.

4. Manuel Pedro González, "Leopoldo Marechal y la novela fantástica," *Cuadernos americanos*, 151 (1967), 204.

5. "Ciclopropano," *Tapioca Inn* (México: Tezontle, 1952), p. 96.

6. "Du réalisme a la réalité," *Pour un nouveau roman* (Paris: Gallimard, 1963), p. 171.

7. Rev. of *La noche*, by Juan García Ponce, *La cultura en México*, No. 84 [Suppl. *Siempre!*] (septiembre 25, 1963), p. xix.

8. Arreola, interviewed by Emmanuel Carballo, *19 protagonistas de la literatura mexicana del siglo XX* (México: Empresas Editoriales, 1965), pp. 400–401.

9. Ibid., p. 367.

10. Arreola, interviewed by Mauricio de la Selva, *Diálogos con América* (México: Cuadernos Americanos, 1964), p. 31.

11. Published in *Revista de la Universidad de México*, 19, No. 10 (1967), 9–11.

12. Arreola, in *19 protagonistas* . . ., p. 376.

13. Arreola, interviewed by Beatriz Espejo, "Confesiones de Arreola," *Ovaciones*, Suppl. No. 147 (octubre 18, 1964), p. 2.

14. Fuentes, interviewed by Emmanuel Carballo, *19 protagonistas* . . ., p. 429.

15. "En defensa de la Trigolibia," *Los días enmascarados* (México: Los Presentes, 1954), p. 29.

16. Fuentes, in *19 protagonistas* . . ., p. 430.

17. "En defensa de la Trigolibia," p. 30.

18. Idem.

19. Albert Camus, *The Myth of Sisyphus*, trans. Justin O'Brien (New York: Vintage Books, 1955), p. 5.

NOTES TO CHAPTER VII

1. Bernard S. Myers, *Expressionism: a Generation in Revolt* (London: Thames and Hudson, 1963), p. 228.

2. Ibid., p. 229.

3. Quoted by Fritz Schmalenbach, "The Term 'Neue Sachlichkeit'," *The Art Bulletin,* 22, No. 3 (Sept. 1940), 161.

4. *Nach-Expressionismus: Magischer Realismus* (Leipzig: Klinkhardt and Biermann, 1925). Spanish version: *Realismo mágico,* trans. Fernando Vela (Madrid: Revista de Occidente, 1927).

5. "El cuento venezolano," *Letras y hombres de Venezuela,* (México: Fondo de Cultura Económica, 1948), pp. 161–162.

6. "Verdad en la ficción," *El heroismo intelectual* (México: Tezontle, 1955), p. 135. The essay was originally published in 1952.

7. "Magical Realism in Spanish American Fiction," *Hispania,* 38, No. 2 (May 1955), 187–192; "El realismo mágico en la ficción narrativa his-panoamericana," *Et Caetera,* 6, Nos. 23–25 (1957–58), 99–108.

8. Idem.

9. Quoted by Juan Eduardo Cirlot, *Diccionario de los ismos* (Barcelona: Argos, 1949), p. 365.

10. "El realismo mágico en la literatura hispanoamericana," *Cuadernos americanos,* 152 (1967), 230–235.

11. Ibid., pp. 232–233. One could have expected this lucid article to fix the meaning of "magical realism" and thus prevent further confusion. Nevertheless, two years later, the Venezuelan critic Pablo Rojas Guardia published a book entitled *La realidad mágica* (Caracas: Monte Avila Editores, 1969), a collection of essays on authors including Ciro Alegría, Mario Vargas Llosa, and Eduardo Mallea with magical realism being the sort of experimentation with time found in Proust and Joyce. Again in 1969 and in the same periodical as Leal's work—which he evidently did not read—Ángel Valbuena Briones published an article "Una cala en el realismo mágico," *Cuadernos americanos,* 166 (1969), 233–241, based on the well-known but dubious study by Ángel Flores.

12. "Hearing the Scream," *Atlas: A Window on the World,* 14, No. 6 (Dec. 1967), 58.

13. "Magical Realism and the Literary World of Miguel Angel Asturias," Unpublished Ph.D. dissertation, University of Washington, 1965, p. 17.

14. "El ídolo en el atrio," *Los mejores poemas de José Juan Tablada,* ed. J. M. González de Mendoza (México: Editorial "Surco", 1943), p. 102.

15. "Tlactocatzine, del jardín de Flandes," *Los días enmascarados* (México: Los Presentes, 1954), pp. 48–50.

16. *Aura,* 2a ed. (México: Ediciones Era, 1964), p. 9.

17. With respect to this influence of Butor, it is well to note that lack of originality in narrative technique is not necessarily a deficiency. Other influences recognized in *Aura* include the title, probably borrowed from one of

Fuente's favorite authors—the controversial José María Vargas Vila (*Aura o las violetas* [Maracaibo, Venezuela, 1887; also México, 1951]), and the essential plot so like that of "La cena" (1920), an excellent and widely-anthologized fantasy by Alfonso Reyes. In "La cena" the narrator goes to a strange house to keep a nine o'clock dinner engagement with people he has never met. Two women receive him and after dinner they show him into the garden and then, oddly, they beg him to describe the city of Paris for the enjoyment of the elder lady's dead husband, a former Captain of Artillery, who is present only in the form of a photograph. When the narrator looks at the picture of the Captain, he is terrified and runs out of the house because the face he sees is his own. As he reaches home the clock is just striking nine, yet it cannot have been a dream for in his buttonhole is a flower from that garden.

18. Carlos Fuentes, interviewed by Emmanuel Carballo, 19 *protagonistas de la literatura mexicana del siglo XX* (México: Empresas Editoriales, 1965), pp. 427–428.

19. "De lo real maravillosamente americano," *Tientos y diferencias: ensayos* (México: Universidad Nacional Autónoma de México, 1964), pp. 133–134, 135.

20. Excerpt from a personal letter from Torres Septién, dated October 13, 1967.

21. "La retro" was written by Reyes in 1931 but only published in *Árbol de pólvora* (México: Imprenta Nuevo Mundo, 1953); Alejo Carpentier's story "Viaje a la semilla" first appeared in a very limited edition of one hundred copies (La Habana: Ucar García y Cía., 1944). Salvador Bueno included it in his *Antología del cuento en Cuba (1902–1952)* (La Habana, 1953), but it only became widely known when republished by Carpentier in *Guerra del tiempo* (México: Cía. General de Ediciones, 1958). In any case, the reversibility of time has been a familiar theme in literature ever since Plato's Eleatic Stranger described to the Younger Socrates the ancient tradition according to which, at the completion of a certain cycle, God ceased to direct the world in its accustomed course. Thus released, the world began to move spontaneously in an opposite direction. See *The Dialogues of Plato*, trans. B. Jowett (New York: Random House, 1937), II, 296–302. The probable Irano-Babylonian origin of the myth of cosmic regression is traced by Mircea Eliade in his *The Myth of the Eternal Return or, Cosmos and History*, trans. Willard R. Trask (Princeton, N.J.: Princeton University Press, 1971), pp. 120–122.

22. T. S. Eliot, "Ulysses, Order and Myth," *The Dial*, 75 (1923), 483.

23. "La ciudad fantasma," *Juego de espejos* (México: Imprenta Universitaria, 1959), p. 29.

24. "Luvina," *El llano en llamas*, 6a ed. (México: Fondo de Cultura Económica, 1964), p. 104.

25. "Realidad y estilo de Juan Rulfo," *Revista mexicana de literatura*, 1, No. 1 (1957), 155.

26. Luis Leal, "El realismo mágico . . .," p. 235.

Bibliography

Entries are arranged alphabetically by author. Each entry includes whenever possible the following data: author, author's dates, title of the work, genre, collection in which published, place, publisher, and date of publication. Place of publication for all periodicals cited is Mexico City unless otherwise noted. Books by the same author are listed in order of publication. Details of original publication are also given for all items that appeared in print before being gathered into a volume.

BIBLIOGRAPHY

Acosta Enríquez, José Mariano (before 1779–after 1816). *Sueño de sueños* [novel]. Biblioteca del Estudiante Universitario, Núm. 55. México: Imprenta Universitaria, 1945 [written c. 1800].

Aguilar, Gilberto F. (1888–1959). *Diez cuentos* [short stories]. México: [Ediciones Botas], 1936: El fusilado.

Aguilar, Jorge. *Ecce homo* [short stories]. Los Presentes, Núm. 31. México, 1955: Tránsito.—El ascenso.—Roma.—Ecce homo.

Alvardo, José (1911–1974). *Memorias de un espejo* [novelette]. México: Chimalístac, 1953.

————. *El personaje* [novelette]. Los Presentes, Núm. 16. México, 1955.

Alvarado Fernández, Valdemar. "Dos teletransportaciones y un sueño" [short story]. "Revista de la semana," Suppl. *El universal*, junio 30, 1968, p.4.

Arellano, Angel R. de. *Leyendas y tradiciones relativas a las calles de México* [legends]. México: J. J. Terrazas e Hijo, Impresores, 1894: Leyenda de la Calle de Olmedo.

Arredón Ramos, Arturo. *Mosaicos negros* [novel]. Guadalajara, Jalisco: Talleres Linotipográficos Morales, 1959.

Arreola, Juan José (1918). *Varia invención* [short stories]. México: Tezontle, 1949: Un pacto con el diablo [First published in *Letras de México*, 4, No. 7 (julio 15, 1943), 10].—El silencio de Dios [First published in *Letras de México*, 4, No. 12 (diciembre 15, 1943), 9–10].—El soñado.—Pablo [First published in *Cuadernos americanos*, 41, No. 6 (noviembre–diciembre 1947), 239–248].—La migala.

————. *Cuentos* [short stories]. Los Presentes, 1a Ser., Núm. 4. México, 1950: El lay de Aristóteles.—Apuntes de un rencoroso.

————. *Confabulario* [short stories]. Letras Mexicanas, Núm. 2. México: Fondo de Cultura Económica, 1955 [Reprinted: all of *Cuentos*]: En verdad os digo.—El guardagujas.—La caverna.—Pueblerina.—Autrui.—El prodigioso miligramo.—El condenado.—Baby H. P.—Prosodia [Includes: Topos.—Insectiada.—Libertad.—El diamante].

————. *Confabulario y varia invención (1941–1955)* [short stories]. Segunda edición conjunta. Letras Mexicanas, Núm. 2. México: Fondo de Cultura Económica, 1955 [Reprinted: All of *Varia invención* and *Confabulario*]: Parturient montes [First published in *Nuestros cuentos*, 2a Ser., Colección Tehutli, Núm. 4. México: Unidad Mexicana de Escritores, 1955, pp. 109–112].—Parábola del trueque [First published in *Ideas de México*, Año 5, 2a Ser., 2, Nos. 9–10 (enero-abril 1955)].—Una mujer amaestrada.—El mapa de los objetos perdidos.—Flash.—Luna de miel.

————. *Confabulario total (1941–1961)* [short stories]. Letras Mexicanas. México: Fondo de Cultura Económica, 1962 [Reprinted: all of *Confabulario y varia invención (1941–1955)*]: Inferno V.—Informe de Liberia.—Una de dos.—Tú y yo.—Caballero desarmado. [These five stories first published as "Prosodia" in *Revista mexicana de literatura*, n.s., No. 4 (octubre 1959), 1–8].—Anuncio [First published in "La cultura en México," No. 4, Suppl.

Siempre!, marzo 14, 1962, pp. iv–v.—Alarma para el año 2000.—Homenaje a Otto Weininger.—La trampa.—De *L'osservatore*.

——————. *Confabulario* [short stories]. Colección Popular, Núm. 80. México: Fondo de Cultura Económica, 1966 [Reprinted: All of *Confabulario total (1941–1961)*]: *Loco dolente.*—El rey negro.—*Kalenda maya.* [These stories first published among "Textos" in *Revista de bellas artes*, No. 3 (mayo-junio 1965), 17–27].

——————. "Starring: All People" [short story]. *Revista de la Universidad de México*, 21, No. 10 (junio 1967), 9–11.

Atl, Dr. [pseud. of Gerardo Murillo] (1874–1964). *Un hombre más allá del universo* [narrative essay]. México: Ediciones Botas, 1935.

——————. *Cuentos de todos colores* [short stories]. Vol. I. México: Ediciones Botas, 1933: El asesino.

——————. *Cuentos de todos colores* [short stories]. Vol. II. México: Ediciones Botas, 1936: La barra de metal.—El reló del muerto.—Acción a distancia.

——————. *El Padre Eterno, Satanás y Juanito García* [novel]. México: Ediciones Botas, 1938.

——————. *Cuentos de todos colores* [short stories]. Vol. III. México: Ediciones Botas, 1941: El aullido de la Llorona.—El hombre que se quedó ciego en el espacio.

Avalos Ficacci, Rafael. "Fábulas con moraleja" [short story]. *El cuento: revista de imaginación*, 3, No. 14 (julio-agosto 1965), 43–45.

——————. "Relatividad" [short story]. *El cuento: revista de imaginación*, 4, No. 25 (agosto 1967), 648–649.

Balbontín, Manuel (1824–1894). *Memorias de un muerto: cuento fantástico* [novel]. México: Imprenta en la Calle de Tiburicio, número 7, 1874.

Balbuena, Bernardo de (1561?–1627). *Siglo de oro en las selvas de Erífile* [novel]. Madrid: Imprenta Alonso Martín, 1608.

Banda Farfán, Raquel (1928). *Escenas de la vida rural* [short stories]. México, 1953: Un viaje al más allá.—Noche de brujas.

——————. *El secreto* [short stories]. México: Editorial Diana, 1960: En la laguna.

——————. *Amapola* [short stories]. México: B. Costa-Amic, Editor, 1964: La hechicera.

Barragán T., R. "Om" [short story]. "Revista de la semana," Suppl. *El universal*, junio 9, 1968, p. 4.

Barreda, Octavio G. (1897–1964). *El Dr. Fu Chang Li* [short story]. Colección "Lunes," Núm. 9. México: Pablo y Henrique González-Casanova; Imprenta de B. Costa-Amic, 1945.

Barreto, Virginia. *Juego de sombras y otros relatos* [short stories]. México: Editorial Stylo, 1944: Juego de sombras.—El retorno.—Milagro inútil.—Fosforescencia.—Microcosmos.

Batiza, Sarah (1914). "La ranita verde" [short story]. *Anuario del cuento mexicano 1962*. México: Instituto Nacional de Bellas Artes, 1963. Pp. 41–45.

Becerra Acosta, Manuel (1881–1968). *Los domadores y otras narraciones* [short stories]. México: Ediciones Excélsior, 1945: Los domadores.—Nosotros los perros.—El vendedor de venganzas.—El laboratorio de espíritus. —Maternidad.—La tragedia de los inmortales.—El negro que se pintó de negro.

Benítez, Fernando (1911). *Caballo y Dios: relatos sobre la muerte* [short stories]. Colección Antares. México: Editorial Leyenda, 1945: Un extraño personaje.

Bermúdez, María Elvira (1916). *Soliloquio de un muerto* [short story]. Colección Los Epígrafes, Núm. 10. México, 1951.

—————. "Así es morir" [short story]. "Revista mexicana de cultura," No. 309, Suppl. *El nacional*, marzo 1, 1953, pp. 8–9.

—————. "Alegoría presuntuosa" [short story]. *América: revista antológica*, No. 68 (marzo 1953), 133–139.

—————. "El inútil velorio" [short story]. "México en la cultura," Suppl. *Novedades* [1953?].

—————. "La partida" [short story]. "México en la cultura," Suppl. *Novedades* [1953?].

—————. "En el umbral de la Gloria" [short story]. "Revista mexicana de cultura," No. 435, Suppl. *El nacional*, julio 31, 1955, pp. 8–9.

—————. "La búsqueda" [short story]. *Anuario del cuento mexicano 1959*. México: Instituto Nacional de Bellas Artes, 1960. Pp. 22–28 [Not published elsewhere].

—————. "El regreso" [short story]. *Anuario del cuento mexicano 1962*. México: Instituto Nacional de Bellas Artes, 1963. Pp. 52–55 [Not published elsewhere].

—————. "Agujeros en la nada" [short story]. "Revista mexicana de cultura," No. 946, Suppl. *El nacional*, mayo 16, 1965, p. 5.

—————. "Desde Sorrento" [short story]. "Diorama de la cultura," Suppl. *Excélsior*, noviembre 21, 1965, p. 6.

—————. "Lo que atares en la tierra . . ." [short story]. "Revista mexicana de cultura," No. 979, Suppl. *El nacional*, enero 2, 1966, p. 2.

—————. "La oscuridad primordial" [short story]. "Diorama de la cultura," Suppl. *Excélsior*, abril 24, 1966, pp. 5,6.

—————. "La Casa de los Tiestos" [short story]. "Diorama de la cultura," Suppl. *Excélsior*, mayo 22, 1966, p. 5.

—————. "En espiral" [short story]. "Diorama de la cultura," Suppl. *Excélsior*, diciembre 10, 1967, p. 6.

—————. "Hespéride" [short story]. "Revista mexicana de cultura," No. 1084, Suppl. *El nacional*, enero 7, 1968, p. 7.

——————. "La conversión" [short story]. "Suplemento cultural," No. 7, 5a Ser., *El nacional*, mayo 5, 1968, p.12.

——————. [Note: See also under pseud. Raúl Weil].

Bernal, Rafael (1915–1972). *Su nombre era muerte* [novel]. México: Editorial Jus, 1947.

Betancourt, Fray Agustín de (1620–1700). *Teatro mexicano: descripción breve de los sucesos ejemplares, históricos, políticos, militares y religiosos del Nuevo Mundo Occidental de las Indias* [legends]. México, 1698: Nuestra Señora del Valle.

Bolaños, Joaquín. *La portentosa vida de la Muerte, Emperatriz de los Sepulcros, Vengadora de los Agravios del Altísimo, y muy Señora de la Humana Naturaleza* [novel]. México: Herederos del Lic. D. Joseph de Jauregui, 1792.

Bolio de Peón, Dolores (1880). "El Cristo de las ampollas" [legend]. *Imaginación de México*, ed. Rafael Heliodoro Valle. Colección Austral, Núm. 477. Buenos Aires y México: Espasa-Calpe, 1945, pp. 168–170.

Bonifaz Nuño, Alberto (1911). *Juego de espejos* [short stories]. México: Imprenta Universitaria, 1959: La ciudad fantasma.—El gnomo.—Desdoblamiento.—La cuerda floja.—El golpear de la fragua [First published in *Letras de México*, 10, No. 121 (marzo 1, 1946), 235–236].

——————. "La llave maestra" [short story]. *Anuario del cuento mexicano 1961*. México: Instituto Nacional de Bellas Artes, 1962. Pp. 56–59. [First published in *Cuadernos del viento*, 2, No. 20 (marzo 1962), 289–290].

——————. "La estatuilla de piedra" [short story]. *Cuadernos del viento*, 4, Nos. 43–44 (mayo–junio 1964), 682–684.

Bramón, Francisco (died after 1654). *Los sirgueros de la Virgen sin original pecado* [novel]. México: Imprenta del Lic. Juan de Alcazar, 1620.

Bravo Castillo, Sergio. "Mi experiencia con los burococos" [short story]. "Revista de la semana," Suppl. *El universal*, junio 16, 1968, p.4.

Cabada, Juan de la (1903). *Paseo de mentiras* [short stories]. Colección Lucero. México: Editorial Séneca, 1940: María, "La Voz" [First published in *Taller*, 1, No. 6 (noviembre 1939), 24–43].

Cadena Z[epeda], Daniel (1914). . . . *por el ojo de la aguja* . . . [novel]. México, 1961.

——————. *La aguja en el pajar* [novel]. México, 1962.

Calvillo Madrigal, Salvador (1901). *Adán, el importante* [short stories]. Colección Stylo de Escritores Mexicanos Antiguos y Modernos. México: Editorial Stylo, 1952: Tabú.—El baldado, y otras cosas.—Azul.—El hombre que robó a la Muerte [First published in *El hijo pródigo*, 12, No. 38 (mayo 1946), 91–95].

——————. "El Señor Aquél" [short story]. *Anuario del cuento mexicano 1959*. México: Instituto Nacional de Bellas Artes, 1960. Pp. 35–39 [First published in *Nivel*, No. 2 (febrero 25, 1959), 6].

Camarena M[achorro], Pedro. *El mundo que soñamos* [novel]. México: Editorial "EME," 1956.

Campos, Rubén M[aría] (1876–1945). "El dictado del muerto" [short story]. *Revista moderna*, 4, No. 2 (abril 1–15, 1901), 106–108.

Cañedo, Diego [pseud. of Guillermo Zárraga] (1892). *El réferi cuenta nueve* [novel]. México: Editorial Cultura, 1943.

—————— . *Palamás, Echevete y yo (o el lago asfaltado)* [novel]. México: Editorial Stylo, 1945.

—————— . *La noche anuncia el día* [novel]. México: Editorial Stylo, 1947.

—————— . *El extraño caso de una litografía mexicana* [short story]. México: Editorial Stylo, 1948.

—————— . *La historia del pequeño fauno de Chelsea* [short story]. México: Editorial Stylo, 1951.

—————— . *Isolda (o el misterio de las gafas verdes)* [short story]. México: Editorial Stylo, 1952.

—————— . *El presente de Ariel* [short story]. México: Editorial Stylo, 1954.

—————— . *Vida, expiación y muerte de Arístides Elorrio* [short story]. México: Editorial Stylo, 1956.

—————— . *El milagro* [short story]. México: Imprenta de Manuel Casas, 1963.

—————— . "El Jueves Santo de Julio Argudín" [short story]. Madrid, 1964.

—————— . "La singular aventura de Agustín Monterde" [short story]. [unpublished; written 1950].

—————— . "Non fecit taliter omni nationi" [short story]. [unpublished; written February 1953].

—————— . "Lilith" [short story]. [unpublished; written June 1963.].

—————— . "La vida increíble de Julián Churruca" [novel]. [unpublished].

—————— . "El caso de los billetes volatilizados" [short story]. [unpublished; written August 1967].

Cardeña, Jaime (1920). *El dominó* [short stories]. Pájaro Cascabel, Núm. 4. México, 1964: Charles Darwin IV.—El fin del sueño.—Amazonas Inc.—Compagnie de Voyages Montgolfier.—Conócete a ti mismo.—Sorcerer's Apprentice.—El epitalamio de Onésimo Segundo [First published in *Cuadernos de bellas artes*, 3, No. 9 (septiembre 1962), 19–20].—La tarde del mundo.

—————— . "El hombre del caftán" [short story]. *El cuento: revista de imaginación*, 5, No. 27 (diciembre 1967), 209–212.

Cardona Peña, Alfredo (1917). *Cuentos de magia, de misterio y de horror* [short stories]. Colección Relatos Extraordinarios, Núm. 1. México y París: Alejandro Finisterre, Editor, 1966: La otra muerte.—El muro.—La camelia.—El hombre que vio.—Trompetas y gallos.—Un cuadro en la Eternidad.—Más allá, también más allá [First published in *Aventura y misterio (originales en castellano)*, Vol. X. México: Editorial Novaro-México, 1957, pp. 23–40].—El mejor cuento de misterio [First published in *Cuadernos de bellas artes*, 3, No. 12 (diciembre 1962), 22–32].—Epílogo del cuento anterior.—Origen de la nostalgia.—El jardín de los puñales en flor.—Tres golpes en la puerta.—Testigo ocular.—Historia de Akbar y Lasur.—El rey de los magos.—Una vez al año.—La niña de Cambridge.—Detrás del silencio.—Los homoglobitas.—Cíclopes.—Un interesante reportaje.—La lluvia de oro.

——————. "Una noticia en el álbum" [short story]. "México en la cultura," No. 940, Suppl. Novedades, marzo 26, 1967, pp. 5,8.

——————. "Contraorden" [short story]. México en la cultura," No. 994, Suppl. Novedades, abril 7, 1968, p. 5.

Carrancá y Rivas, Raúl (1930). El mundo al revés [short stories]. México: Colección "Voces Nuevas," 1953: El mundo al revés.—Los hombres de los dos cuartos.—Angustia.—Muchos son los llamados pero pocos los elegidos.—Parábola del artista.—El judío errante.—La verdadera historia de José.

Castillo, Clemencia del. "El mensajero misterioso" [short story]. "Revista de la semana," Suppl. El universal, septiembre 15, 1968, pp. 4–5.

Castillo Ledón, Beatriz. Rubicundo Hematíes [novelette]. México, 1962.

Castro Leal, Antonio (1896). El laurel de San Lorenzo [short stories]. Letras Mexicanas, Núm. 56. México: Fondo de Cultura Económica, 1959: El espía del alma [First published in Revista de la Universidad de México, 10, No. 4 (diciembre 1955), 6–8].—El coleccionista de almas [First published in Panoramas (Galerías Excélsior), B. Costa-Amic, Editor, No. 1 (primavera 1956), 123–146].—La literatura no se cotiza [First published in Letras de México, 1, No. 2 (febrero 1, 1937), 6].—Una historia del siglo XX [First published in Cuadernos americanos, 83, No. 5 (septiembre–octubre 1955), 265–289].

Castro Leal, Antonio, hijo. Susamar [short story]. Cuadernos Literarios Lince, Núm. 2. México: Impresiones Modernas, 1956.

Ceballos, Ciro B. (1873–1938). "El guantelete" [short story]. Revista moderna, 2, No. 1, (enero 1899), 121–123.

Cele. "La deuda" [short story]. "Revista de la semana," Suppl. El universal, julio 28, 1968, pp. 4–5.

Colina, José de la (1934). Ven, caballo gris [short stories]. Colección Ficción, Núm. 10. Xalapa, Veracruz: Universidad Veracruzana, 1959: El tercero [First published in Revista mexicana de literatura, 1, No. 6 (julio–agosto 1956), 596–605].

Collantes y Buenrostro, Juan (1849–1916). Leyendas fantásticas [legends]. México: Imprenta y Litografía de Ireneo Paz, 1877.

Couto, José Bernardo (1803–1862). Obras del doctor D. José Bernardo Couto, I, Opúsculos varios. Biblioteca de Autores Mexicanos, Núm. 13. México: Imprenta de V[ictoriano] Agüeros, Editor, 1898: La mulata de Córdoba.—La historia de un peso [short stories]. [First published (together) in Calendario antiguo (1882)].

Couto Castillo, Bernardo (1880–1901). "Celos póstumos" [short story]. Revista moderna, 1, No. 7 (noviembre 1, 1898), 107–108.

Cruz M., Gustavo. "Los fantasmas" [short story]. El cuento: revista de imaginación, Año 2, Tomo 3, No. 13 (junio 1965), 507–510.

—————— . "Gulliver" [short story]. *El cuento: revista de imaginación,* Año 3, Tomo 3, No. 17 (octubre 1966), 394–395.

Cuevas, Alejandro (1870–1940). *Cuentos macabros* [short stories]. Prologue by Juan de Dios Peza. México: Librería Central; J. R. Garrido y Hermano, Editores, 1911: Ante el jurado.—El fin de Mariana [First published in "Suplemento ilustrado," Suppl. *El diario,* octubre 11, 1908. p. 3].—Carboncillo [First published in "Suplemento ilustrado," Suppl. *El diario,* octubre 25, 1908, p. 8].—La escultura de cera.—El aparato del Doctor Tolimán.—Cordelia.

Dávila, [María] Amparo (1928). *Tiempo destrozado* [short stories]. Letras Mexicanas, Núm. 46. México: Fondo de Cultura Económica, 1959: Fragmento de un diario (julio–agosto) [First published as "Fragmentos de diario de un masoquista (julio–agosto)" in *12 cuentistas potosinos contemporáneos.* San Luis Potosí: Unión de Escritores y Periodistas de San Luis Potosí, 1959. Pp. 113–122].—El huésped [First published in *Revista mexicana de literatura,* 2a Ser., 1, No. 6 (julio–agosto 1956), 565–570].—La quinta de las celosías.—La celda.—Final de una lucha.—Tiempo destrozado.—El espejo [First published in *Letras potosinas,* San Luis Potosí, Nos. 121–22 (julio–diciembre 1956), 36–38].—Moisés y Gaspar [First published in *Revista mexicana de literatura,* 2a Ser., 2, No. 12 (julio–agosto 1957), 27–35; and in *Cuadrante* (Universidad Autónoma de San Luis Potosí), 5, Nos. 1–4 (1957), 36–46].

—————— . *Música concreta* [short stories]. Letras Mexicanas, Núm. 79. México: Fondo de Cultura Económica, 1964: El jardín de las tumbas.—Música concreta.—El entierro [First published in *Revista de la Universidad de México,* 15, No. 6 (febrero 1961), 7–10].

—————— . "Arboles petrificados" [short stories]. *Diálogos,* 2, No. 6 (octubre–noviembre 1966), 15–16.

Delhumeau, Eduardo. *El año 3000 bis* [novel]. México: Ediciones Ybarra, 1945.

Dueñas, Guadalupe (1920). "Tres cuentos" [short stories]. *Abside,* 19, No. 1 (enero–marzo 1955), 64–75: Diplodocus sapiens.

—————— . *Tiene la noche un árbol* [short stories]. Letras Mexicanas, Núm. 41. México: Fondo de Cultura Económica, 1958: Tiene la noche un árbol.—Historia de Mariquita [First published in *Revista de la Universidad de México,* 9, No. 8 (abril 1955), 6,10].—Al roce de la sombra.—La hora desteñida [First published in *Abside,* 20, No. 2 (abril–junio 1956), 199–202].—Mi chimpancé [First published in "Las ratas y otros cuentos," *Abside,* 17, No. 3 (julio–septiembre 1954), 337–349].—Y se abrirá el Libro de la Vida [Much revised version of "Juicio final," *Revista mexicana de literatura,* 2a Ser., 2, Nos. 9–10 (enero–abril 1957), 3–6].—Caso clínico [First published in *Abside,* 19, No. 3 (julio–septiembre 1955), 384–386; and in *Poesía de América,* 3, No. 6 (julio–agosto–septiembre 1955), 28–30].

Durán Rosado, Esteban (1905). *Marcela* [short stories]. Biblioteca de Literatura Mexicana. México: Editorial Castalia, 1963: La muerte verdadera [First published in "Revista de la semana," Suppl. *El universal,* mayo 14, 1961, pp. 3–4, 7].—El hijo del mar.

Echenique, Gabriel. "El Secretero" [short story]. *12 cuentistas potosinos contemporáneos.* San Luis Potosí: Unión de Escritores y Periodistas de San Luis Potosí, 1959. Pp. 129–138.

Elizondo, Salvador (1932). "Sila" [short story]. *Revista de la Universidad de México,* 17, No. 2 (octubre 1962), 14–16.

——————. *Narda o el verano* [short stories]. Colección Alacena. México: Ediciones Era, 1966: En la playa [First published in *Cuadernos del viento,* 5, Nos. 45–46 (julio–agosto 1964), 713–716].—Narda o el verano.—La puerta [First published in *Revista de bellas artes,* No. 8 (marzo–abril 1966), 37–40].—La historia según Pao Cheng.

——————. "El ángel azul" [short story]. *Cuadernos del viento,* 5, Nos. 59–60 (mayo 1966–enero 1967), 1035–1036.

Escobar, Fray Matías de (b. 1680?). *Americana Thebaida* [legends]. México: Fray Manuel de los Angeles Castro, 1924: Un enemigo del diablo.

Espejo, Beatriz (1937). "El retorno" [short story]. *Anuario del cuento mexicano 1960.* México: Instituto Nacional de Bellas Artes, 1961. Pp. 103–104 [First published in *Cuadernos del viento,* 1, No. 5 (diciembre 1960), 66].

——————. "En mi vigilia" [short story]. *Anuario del cuento mexicano 1961.* México: Instituto Nacional de Bellas Artes, 1962. Pp. 103–105 [First published in *El rehilete,* No. 5 (junio 1962), 18–21].

——————. "La redención" [short story]. *El rehilete,* No. 7 (febrero 1963), 23–24.

Fábregas, J. J. "El error" [short story]. *El cuento: revista de imaginación,* 4, No. 20 (enero–febrero 1967), 55, 57.

Fernández MacGregor, Genaro (1883–1959). *Novelas triviales* [short stories]. Biblioteca Nueva España. México: Andrés Botas e Hijo, Editores, [1918]: En la orla del misterio.—Un mulus ex-machina.

Ferrel [y Félix], José (1865–1954). "Un viaje al cielo" and "La estatua del condenado" [short stories]. *Cuentos mexicanos* [anthology]. México: Tipografía de "El Nacional," 1898. Pp. 69–91 and 225–231, respectively.

Ferretis, Jorge (1902–1962). *Hombres en tempestad* [short stories]. México: Editorial Cima, 1941: Aire [Reprinted as "El viento y las autobiografías" in *Anuario del cuento mexicano 1960.* México: Instituto Nacional de Bellas Artes, 1961. Pp. 105–110].

Frías, Valentín (1862–1926). *Leyendas y tradiciones queretanas* [legends]. 1a Ser. Querétaro: Imprenta de la Escuela de Artes y Oficios del Señor San José, 1900: La cruz de los milagros.—La Patrona de Querétaro [Both stories first published in *El tiempo ilustrado,* México].

Fuentes, Carlos (1928). "Pantera en jazz" [short story]. *Ideas de México,* 2a Ser., 1, No. 3 (enero–febrero 1954), 119–124.

——————. *Los días enmascarados* [short stories]. Los Presentes, Núm. 2. México, 1954: Chac Mool [First published in *Revista de la Universidad de México,* 8, No. 12 (agosto 1954), 7–9].—En defensa de la Trigolibia.—Tlactocatzine, del jardín de Flandes.—Letanía de la orquídea.—Por boca de los dioses.—El que inventó la pólvora.

——————. "El trigo errante" [short story]. *Revista de la Universidad de México,* 11, No. 1 (septiembre 1956), 8–9.

——————. *Aura* [novelette]. Colección Alacena. México: Ediciones Era, 1962.

——————. *Cantar de ciegos* [short stories]. Serie del Volador. México: Editorial Joaquín Mortiz, 1964: La muñeca reina [First published in "La cultura en México," No. 123, Suppl. *Siempre!*, junio 24, 1964, pp. ii–vi].

Gallardo Topete, Salvador (1933). "El gusano que compró a un hombre" [short story]. *ACA: revista de la Asociación Cultural de Aguascalientes* (Aguascalientes), No. 3 (agosto 1954).

Gally C., Héctor (1942). *Diez días y otras narraciones* [short stories]. México: Editorial Pax-México; Librería Carlos Césarman, 1963: La muerte ahorcada. —Después del fin.—El sepulcro.

——————. *Hacia la noche: cuentos* [short stories]. México: B. Costa-Amic, Editor, 1965: La vieja carne.—La carne nueva.

García Cuevas, G. A. "Andrés Bomar" [short story]. "Revista de la semana," Suppl. *El universal*, mayo 5, 1968, p. 4.

García Rodríguez, José (1875–1948). *Relatos: misterio y realismo* [short stories]. México: Editorial Jus, 1947: Misterio.—Jesusín.—La casa de los espantos.—Rediviva.

Garro, Elena (1920). *Los recuerdos del porvenir* [novel]. Novelistas Contemporáneos. México: Editorial Joaquín Mortiz, 1963.

——————. *La semana de colores* [short stories]. Colección Ficción, Núm. 58. Xalapa, Veracruz: Universidad Veracruzana, 1964: La culpa es de los tlaxcaltecas [First published in *Revista mexicana de literatura*, n.s., Nos. 3–4 (marzo–abril 1964), 12–28].—¿Qué hora es . . .? [First published in *Diálogos*, 1, No. 1 (noviembre–diciembre 1964), 18–23].—La semana de colores.—El duende [First published in *Revista de la Universidad de México*, 13, No. 8 (abril 1964), 21–23].—El anillo.—Perfecto Luna [First published in *Revista de la Universidad de México*, 12, No. 12 (agosto 1958), 7–9].

Garza, Ramiro. *El quinto reino* [short stories]. México, 1966: Los misioneros.

Garza Quesada, Lourdes. *La absurda espera y otros cuentos* [short stories]. México: Editorial B. Costa-Amic, 1961: Escaramuza.—Y, conjunción copulativa.—La absurda espera.—Amigas siempre.—Seguimiento.—El tiempo y un hombre.—El encuentro.

Godoy, Jorge de (1894–1950). *El puñado de rubíes* [short story]. México: Herrero Hnos. Sucesores, 1926 [First published in *El universal*, 1921].

Gómez de la Cortina, José Justo (Conde de la Cortina) (1799–1860): "La Calle de don Juan Manuel" [legend]. *Imaginación de México* [anthology], ed. Rafael Heliodoro Valle. Colección Austral, No. 477. Buenos Aires y México: Espasa-Calpe, 1945. Pp. 186–189 [First published in *Revista mexicana* (1835), 551–560].

Gómez Landero, Humberto. "Cuento psicodélico" [short story]. "México en la cultura," No. 993, Suppl. *Novedades*, marzo 31, 1968, p. 5.

Gómez Mayorga, Ana [María Valverde] de (1878–1954). *Entreabriendo la puerta* [short stories]. México: Editorial "Ideas," 1946: El viaje.—La casa.— La fuga.—El soñador.—La mendiga.—El señor cura.—El encargo.—El es-

pejo.—El mar.—La taza de té.—Una visita.—¿Cuál sería?—Minnie la
cándida.—El tesoro.—La cruz.—Margarita.—La excursión.—El monu-
mento.—El fantasma del mar.—El abuelo.—Isabel.—La puerta.

Gómez Mayorga, Mauricio (1913). "La navegación" [short story]. *Panoramas*
No. 1 (primavera 1956), 147–165.

———. "Poseidonis" [short story]. *Estaciones*, 1, No. 2 (verano 1956),
238–240.

Gómez Robleda, José (1904). *Esquizofrénico* [short story]. México: Imprenta
Mundial, 1933.

———. *Nóumeno* [narrative essays]. México: Imprenta de A. Mijares y
Hno., 1942: Nadie.—¿Qué quiere Ud.?—Nada.—¿Dónde?—Somos.—Fin
final.—Más allá.—Falsedad falsa.—Discusión.

González Obregón, Luis (1865–1938). *Las calles de México: leyendas y suce-
didos* [legends]. Biblioteca Popular de Autores Mexicanos, No. 1. México:
Ediciones León Sánchez, 1922: La Llorona.—Un aparecido: Leyenda de la
Plaza Mayor.—La Calle de D. Juan Manuel.—La Mulata de Córdoba: Suc-
edido en la Calle de la Perpetua.—La hermana de los Avila: Sucedido en la
Calle de la Concepción (ahora la de Belisario Domínguez).—El Santo Ecce
Homo del Portal: Tradición del Portal de Agustinos.—Lo que aconteció a
una monja con un clérigo difunto: Leyenda de la Calle de Jesús María.—La
calle de la mujer herrada: Sucedido de la Calle de la Puerta Falsa de Santo
Domingo (ahora del Perú).

González Pineda, Francisco (1918). *Solimán y otros relatos* [short stories].
México: Cuadernos del Viento, 1961: Chaneques.—Solimán.—Veneno en
tequila [First published in *Cuadernos del viento*, 1, No. 6 (enero 1961),
91–95].

González Rojo, Enrique, hijo (1931). "Un peligro" [short story]. *Anuario del
cuento mexicano 1954*. México: Instituto Nacional de Bellas Artes, 1955.
Pp. 225–230 [First published in *Ideas de México*, 2a Ser., 1, No. 5 (mayo-
–junio 1954), 211–214].

González Vázquez, Jesús. "El billete del diablo" [short story]. "Revista de la
semana," Suppl. *El universal*, septiembre 1, 1968, pp. 4–5.

Grajales, Sergio F. "Un mago tonto" [short story]. "Revista de la semana,"
Suppl. *El universal*, julio 14, 1968, p. 4.

Guerrero, Jesús R. (1911). "Un ensueño posible" [short story]. *Anuario del
cuento mexicano 1954*. México: Instituto Nacional de Bellas Artes, 1955.
Pp. 231–236 [First published in "Revista mexicana de cultura," No. 364,
Suppl. *El nacional*, marzo 21, 1954, p. 4].

Gutiérrez Nájera, Manuel (1859–1895). *Cuentos frágiles* [short stories].
Biblioteca Honrada. México: Imprenta del Comercio de E. Dublán y Cía.,
1883: Las misas de Navidad [First published as "Cosas del mundo (Las
misas de Navidad)" in *El nacional*, diciembre 24, 1880; republished as
"Crónica de Noche Buena" in 1882].—La pasión de Pasionaria [First published as "Cartas de mi abuela" and signed "M. Can-Can" in *El cronista de
México*, julio 9, 1882; republished as "¡Llueve! ¡Llueve!" in 1891 and
1893].—Los amores del cometa [First published among *Crónicas color de
oro* and signed "El Duque Job" in *La libertad*, octubre 1, 1882].—Después

de las carreras [First published as "Crónica de Caracole" in *La libertad*, noviembre 12, 1882; republished as "Berta y Manón" in 1892 and as "Un día de carreras" in *Revista Azul*, 4, No. 17, febrero 23, 1896, pp. 255–257].

——————. *Obras de . . .* (Prosa), Vol. I. Prologue by Luis G. Urbina. México: Tipografía de la Oficina Impresora del Timbre. Palacio Nacional, 1898: Memorias de un paraguas [short story] [First published as "La vida en México (Memorias de un paraguas)" in *La libertad*, junio 3, 1883].—Rip-Rip el aparecido [short story] [First published as "Cuentos vistos (Rip-Rip)" in *El universal*, mayo 11, 1890; included in "Cuentos color de humo," *Revista Azul*, 1, No. 22, septiembre 30, 1894, pp. 347–349].—Dos y uno [short story] [First published as subdivision of his article "Confidencias" in *El federalista*, enero 28, 1877].

Guzmán, Martín Luis (1887). "Cómo acabó la guerra en 1917" [short story]. *El cuento mexicano del siglo XX: antología*, ed. Emmanuel Carballo. México: Empresas Editoriales, 1964. Pp. 191–199 [First published in *Revista universal*, New York (December 1917), 18, 82].

Haydt R., Guillermo. "La noticia" [short story]. "Revista de la semana," Suppl. *El universal*, agosto 25, 1968, ן ־ן. 4–5.

Hernández, María de Lourdes. *En el nuevo Aztlán* [novel]. Sahuayo, Michoacán: Asociación Propulsora del Arte, 1949.

Herrera Carrillo, José Guadalupe (1900–1963). *Juan Garabato y otros "Garabatos"* [short stories]. Guanajuato: Ediciones Llave; Universidad de Guanajuato, 1962: Míster Parkington aprende a reír.—El extraño caso de Raimundo Díaz [First published in *Difusiones*, Guanajuato, No. 4 (1953), 25–35].

Hidalgo, María Luisa (1918). *Cuentas de cuentos* [short stories]. Guadalajara, Jalisco: Ediciones Et Caetera, 1951.

——————. *Renato Camaleón y otros* [short stories]. Guadalajara, Jalisco: Casa de Cultura Jalisciense, 1960: La rata.—Epica del gusano [First published in *Estaciones*, 1, No. 3 (otoño 1956), 358–359].—El cacomixtle.—Renato Camaleón.—Araña [Stories "Renato Camaleón" and "Araña" first published as "Lo cordial de la mentira," *Et caetera* (Guadalajara), 6, Nos. 21–22 (enero–junio 1957)].—La jirafa.—El ornitorrinco.—La fábula del renacuajo.—De Academias.—La cotorra.—La gallina.—El conejo.—La liebre.—La broca.—La víbora.—El encuentro de las estatuas.—Nefertiti y el oso.—La metamorfosis.

Horta, Raúl. *Mariqueta Candela* [short stories]. Epilogue by José Rubén Romero. México: Editorial Stylo, 1947: El hombre que vio a Cristo.—El fraile de Cartago.

Ibarra Mazari, Ignacio (1920). "Una jaula en el balcón" [short story]. *Anuario del cuento mexicano 1962*. México: Instituto Nacional de Bellas Artes, 1963. Pp. 183–192.

Icaza, Xavier (1892–1969). *Panchito Chapopote: relato tropical (o relación de un extraordinario sucedido de la heróica Veracruz)* [novel]. México: Editorial Cultura, 1928.

Jiménez Montellano, Bernardo (1922–1950). *Los títeres y la quiromancia* [short stories]. Colección "Lunes," Núm. 4, México: Pablo y Enrique González-Casanova; Imprenta de B. Costa-Amic, 1945: Los títeres.—La quiromancia.

——————. *El arca del ángel* [short stories]. México: Tezontle, 1952 [Reprinted: "Los títeres"]: Pasanoche.—La enamorada y la muerte.—La mariguana.

Larrea Rionoso, Sergio. "Los vientos sonoros" [short story]. "Revista de la semana, Suppl. *El universal*, junio 2, 1968, p. 4.

Leal Cortés, Alfredo (1931). "Orestes" [short story]. *El cuento mexicano del siglo XX: antología*, ed. Emmanuel Carballo. México: Empresas Editoriales, 1964. Pp. 551–554.

Lilia Rosa [pseud. of Lilia Rosa del Mazo de Groués]. "Actos privativos" [short story]. *Anuario del cuento mexicano 1961*. México: Instituto Nacional de Bellas Artes 1962. Pp. 136–141.

Lille, Paloma de (1938). "Sentada una gata estaba" [short story]. *Cuadernos del viento*, 4, Nos. 37–38 (agosto–diciembre 1963), 592–593.

Lizalde, Eduardo (1929). "Las cadenas" [short story]. *Anuario del cuento mexicano 1955*. México: Instituto Nacional de Bellas Artes, 1956. Pp. 189–196 [First published in *Metáfora*, 1, No. 2 (mayo–junio 1955), 29–34].

——————. *La cámara* [short stories]. México: Imprenta Universitaria, 1960: Maniobras palaciegas [First published in *Cuadernos del viento*, 1, No. 1 (agosto 1960), 6–7].—Cuentos de la Gioconda (I).

López Portillo y Rojas, José (1850–1923). *Novelas cortas* [short stories]. Biblioteca de Autores Mexicanos, Núm. 27. México: Imprenta de V[ictoriano] Agüeros, 1900: El espejo [First published in *La república literaria* (Guadalajara), 2 (1886–1887), 44–57, 65–72].—Adalinda [First published in *La república literaria* (Guadalajara), 3 (1887–1888), 9–21].—Un pacto con el diablo [First published as "La mueca del diablo," in *La república literaria* (Guadalajara), 5 (1889–1890), 634–639, 660–672].

López y Fuentes, Gregorio (1897–1966). *Cuentos campesinos de México* [short stories]. Colección de Autores Mexicanos. México: Editorial "Cima," 1940: La inconformidad.—Un pacto.—El fantasma.—El hombre que miraba en la obscuridad.

Macotela, Fernando (1938). "El último cometa" [short story]. *Anuario del cuento mexicano 1961*. México: Instituto Nacional de Bellas Artes, 1962. Pp. 146–147.

Malo, Luis. *Vida del diablo, o sea breve relato de algunas travesuras que ha hecho en el mundo* [narrative essay]. México: Imprenta de J. R. Barbedillo y Cía.,1876.

Manjarrez, Froylán C. "Los blátidos" [short story]. *El cuento: revista de imaginación*, 4, No. 20 (enero–febrero 1967), 49–51.

——————. "La verdadera historia de Clark Kent" [short story]. *El cuento: revista de imaginación*, 4, No. 20 (enero–febrero 1967), 52, 54.

Marín, Rubén (1910). *El diablo y algo más . . .* [short stories]. México: Editorial Jus, 1964: La piedra. —El ángel.—El crucifijo de mi madre.—El milagro.

Marmolejo, Lucio (1834–1885). *Efemérides guanajuatenses* [legends]. Guanajuato, 1907: La Virgen de Guanajuato.

Melgoza Paralizábal, Arturo. "El consejero nocturno" [short story]. *El cuento: revista de imaginación*, 4, No. 25 (agosto 1967), 683–686.

Melo, Juan Vicente (1932). *La noche alucinada* [short stories]. México: Editorial Fournier; La Prensa Médica Mexicana, 1956: La noche alucinada.— Mi velorio.— Tarántula.

——————. *Fin de semana* [short stories]. Colección Alacena. México: Ediciones Era,1964: La hora inmóvil [First published in *Revista mexicana de literatura*, n.s. Nos. 9–10 (septiembre–octubre 1962), 6–20].

Mendieta y Núñez, Lucio (1895). *La caravana infinita: cuentos y parábolas* [short stories]. México: Editorial Cultura, 1942: El Cristo del milagro.—La parábola del niño pobre.

Mendoza López, Margarita. *. . . de un país inexistente* [short story]. México: Editorial Stylo, 1953.

Meza, Otilia. *La venenosa* [novel]. México: Ediciones "Ego," [1940].

Monterde, Alberto (1923). *Calavera y Jueves Santo* [short stories]. Letras Mexicanas, Núm. 37. México: Fondo de Cultura Económica, 1957: Irma querida.

Monterde, Francisco (1894). *Cuentos mexicanos* [short stories]. Colección Nueva Ercilla. Santiago de Chile: Ediciones Ercilla, 1936: Un anciano judío.—El Bazar.— Un salteador.

——————. *Fábulas sin moraleja y finales de cuentos* [fables]. Prologue by Alfonso Reyes. México: Imprenta Universitaria, 1942 [Seven of the 65 pieces had been published as "Finales de fábulas (de Iriarte)," in *El universal ilustrado*, No. 306, marzo 22, 1923].

——————. *El temor de Hernán Cortés y otras narraciones de la Nueva España* [legends]. Prologue by Luis González Obregón. México: Imprenta Universitaria, 1943: La paloma en el pozo.—El mascarón y el alférez.—El niño de talla indígena.—La cifra maravillosa.—La muerte de don Juan Manuel.

Montilla Duarte, Felipe (1918?). *Cuentos mayas y fantasías* [short stories]. México: Editora Ibero-Americana, 1955: Alma de agua.—Mi gota.—Amnesia.—A.S.B.6: Cuento en prosa rimada.—Xpet: Una visita del más allá.

Mora, Juan Miguel de (1921). *Otra vez el día sexto* [novel]. Novelistas Mexicanos, Núm. 2. México: Editorial Diana, 1967.

Morales Saviñón, Héctor (1920). *Cuentos* [short stories]. México: Imprenta Rafael Dondé, 1940: El camino.—Manzanas podridas.

——————. *Él* [short stories]. México: Ediciones Mexicanas, S. en P., 1946: Las angustias del coco.—El mosquito Patas Largas.

——————. "El país de los cuentos" [short story]. *Nuestros cuentos*, 1a Ser. Colección Tehutli, Núm. 2. México: Unidad Mexicana de Escritores, 1955. Pp. 85–96.

Nervo, Amado (1870–1919). *El donador de almas* [novelette]. Toluca?, México: Ediciones de La Gaceta del Valle," 1904 [First published in 16-page installments with 5 consecutive issues of the Sunday magazine *Cómico*, México, beginning with 3, No. 15, abril 9, 1899].

——————. *Almas que pasan* [short stories]. Madrid: Revista de Archivos, 1906: La última guerra [First published in *El mundo* (1898?)].—Dos rivales [First published in *El mundo* (1898?)].—Las Casas [First published in *El mundo* (1898?)].

——————. *Ellos* [short stories]. París: Sociedad de Ediciones Literarias y Artísticas, [1909]. [Published simultaneously in Vienna: Imprenta de A. Aubin, 1909]: Ellos [First published in *Revista moderna de México*, 2a Ser., 10 (1908), 238–239].—Los que ignoran que están muertos.—Al volver: Alguien ha entrado.—La última diosa (cuento absurdo) [First published in *Revista moderna de México*, 2a Ser., 7 (1906), 118–120].—El del espejo.—Cien años de sueño.

——————. *El diablo desinteresado* [novelette]. *Obras completas*, ed. Alfonso Reyes. XIV. Madrid: Biblioteca Nueva, 1920 [First published in Madrid: *La novela corta*, Núm. 23, 1916].

——————. *El diamante de la inquietud* [novelette]. *Obras completas*, ed. Alfonso Reyes. XIV. Madrid: Biblioteca Nueva, 1920 [First published in Madrid: *La novela corta*, Núm. 62, 1917].

——————. *El sexto sentido* [novelette]. México: "La Novela Semanal" de *El universal ilustrado*, 1918.

——————. *Cuentos misteriosos* [short stories]. *Obras completas*, ed. Alfonso Reyes. XX. Madrid: Biblioteca Nueva, 1921: La novia de Corinto.—El "ángel caído".—Los congelados.—Como en las estampas.—El país en que la lluvia era luminosa.—Los esquifes.—El obstáculo.—El castillo de lo inconsciente.

Núñez y Domínguez, José de Jesús (1887–1959). *Cuentos mexicanos* [short stories]. México: Herrero Hnos. Sucesores, 1925: La llama viviente.

Obregón Espinosa, Jorge. "La pequeña propiedad" [short story]. "México en la cultura," No. 968, Suppl. *Novedades*, octubre 8, 1967, p. 5.

Octavio. ". . . y entró un joven desconocido . . . " [short story]. "Revista de la semana," Suppl. *El universal*, agosto 18, 1968, pp. 4–5.

Ochoa Sandoval, Eglantina (1918?). "Cinco relatos" [short stories]. *Abside*, 16, No. 4 (octubre–diciembre 1952), 477–494: La Sierra.

——————. *Desasimiento* [short stories]. Los Presentes, Núm. 73. México: Ediciones De Andrea, 1959: Muerte tras la pantalla.—Un camión cualquiera.—Una rebelión inusitada.—Tanatos y Eros.

——————. "Flor de sonido" [short story]. *Anuario del cuento mexicano 1959*. México: Instituto Nacional de Bellas Artes, 1960. Pp. 159–162. [Revised and reprinted as "Peperomnia" in *Cuadernos del viento*, 1, No. 3 (octubre 1960), 41–42].

——————. "Breve reseña histórica" [short story]. *Anuario del cuento mexicano 1961*. México: Instituto Nacional de Bellas Artes, 1962. Pp. 178–180.

Oliva, Alberto. *Fantasías: divulgación científica* [narrative essay]. Guadalajara, Jalisco: Talleres Gráficos "Atlas," 1925.

Olivares Carrillo, Armando (1915–1962). *Ejemplario de muertes* [short stories]. Los Presentes, Núm. 59. México, 1957: La ofrenda [First published in *Garabato* (Guanajuato), No. 3 (febrero 1954)].—Quedito, el afortunado [First published in *Garabato*, No. 6 (mayo 1954)].—Los condenados [First published in *Garabato*, Nos. 7–8 (junio–julio 1954)].—Dos versiones sobre Hércules [First published in *Garabato*, No. 4 (marzo 1954)].

Olvera, Carlos. *Mejicanos en el espacio* [novel]. México: Editorial Diógenes, 1968.

Ortiz Avila, Raúl (1906). "Los niños de piedra" [short story]. *Cuentalia: revista de cuentos mexicanos inéditos*, No. 3 (marzo 6, 1953).

Ortiz de Montellano, Bernardo (1899–1949). *Cinco horas sin corazón: entresueños* [short stories]. México: Ediciones de Letras de México, 1940: Cinq-heures-sans-coeur [First published in *Letras de México*, 2, No. 19 (julio 15, 1940), 6, 8].

——————. *El caso de mi amigo Alfazeta* [short stories]. Colección "Lunes," Núm. 21. México: Pablo y Enrique González-Casanova; Imprenta de B. Costa-Amic, 1946: El cabo Muñoz.

Pacheco, José Emilio (1939). *La sangre de Medusa* [short stories]. Cuadernos del Unicornio, Núm. 18. México, 1958: La sangre de Medusa [First published in *Letras nuevas*, 1, No. 4 (julio–agosto 1958), 24–27].—La noche del inmortal.

——————. "Tres ficciones" [short stories]. *La palabra y el hombre* (Xalapa), 4, No. 16 (octubre–diciembre 1960), 155–157: León de Israel.—En el tinglado.—La tortuga.

——————. *El viento distante* [short stories]. Colección Alacena. México: Ediciones Era, 1963: El viento distante [Revised and expanded version of "La tortuga"]. —Parque de diversiones [First published, except for section V, in *Cuadernos del viento*, 3, No. 28 (noviembre 1962), 445–446].

Patiño de Saavedra, Emma. "Tres noches de terror" [short story]. "Revista de la semana," Suppl. *El universal*, agosto 11, 1968, pp. 4–5.

Payno, Manuel (1810–1894). "El diablo y la monja: cuento fantástico" [short story]. *El album mexicano*, 1 (1849), pp. 246–255.

——————. *El fistol del diablo* [novel]. México, 1859 [First published serially in *Revista científica y literaria de Méjico* (Publicada por los Antiguos Redactores del Museo Mejicano): Part I in Tomo 1 (1845), and 11 chaps. of Part II in Tomo 2 (1846), but left incomplete].

Peralta, Oscar. "De vampiros" [short story]. *El cuento: revista de imaginación*, 3, No. 17 (octubre 1966), 360–363.

Pérez Moreno, José (1900). "La Mulata de Córdoba" [legend]. *Imaginación de México*, ed. Rafael Heliodoro Valle. Colección Austral, Núm. 477. Buenos Aires y México: Espasa-Calpe, 1945. Pp. 204–205 [First published in *El universal ilustrado*, México].

Pesado, José Joaquín (1801–1861). "Historia de una peseta, contada por ella misma" [short story]. *El mosaico mexicano*, 3 (1840), 410–413 [The story is signed "P" and is generally attributed to Pesado].

Poniatowska, Elena (1933). *Lilus Kikus* [novelette and short stories]. Los Presentes, Núm. 1. México, 1954: La hija del filósofo.

Prado, Juan José. *Leyendas y tradiciones guanajuatenses* [legends]. León, Guanajuato: Editorial Prado, [1952?]: La Bufa y el pastor.—La Plazuela de los Carcamanes.—La carroza de don M. Campuzano.—Nuestra Señora de Guanajuato.—El Callejón del Infierno.

Prieto, Raúl (1918). *Hueso y carne* [short stories]. Letras Mexicanas, Núm. 28. México: Fondo de Cultura Económica, 1956: Cárcel de muros vivos.—Exito teatral.—Nada.

Ramírez L., Enrique. "El vuelo de prueba" [short story]. "Revista de la sema-na," Suppl. *El universal,* septiembre 8, 1968, pp. 4–5.

Ramos Gómez, Raymundo (1934). *Muerte amurallada* [short stories]. México: Editorial Estaciones, 1958: El día séptimo.—El unicornio de la luna.—El día de Lázaro.—Apuntes del Apocalipsis.

——————. *Enroque de verano (o la partida imposible)* [short story]. Cuadernos del Unicornio, Núm. 11, México, 1958.

Ramos Meza, [José] Ernesto. *Voces de Talpa: historias y leyendas* [legends]. Guadalajara, Jalisco: Tipografía Vera, 1951: La historia de un aparecido.

——————. *La muerte de Pamilo* [novel]. [Guadalajara, Jalisco]: Ediciones Tlacuilo, 1964.

Rendón O., G. "Yonatán Ben Yosef" [short story]. "Revista de la semana," Suppl. *El universal,* mayo 19, 1968, p. 4.

Renner de Cuevas, Ana María. "Cuando todos nos volvimos ricos" [short story]. "Revista de la semana," Suppl. *El universal,* mayo 12, 1968, p. 4.

Reyes, Alfonso (1889–1959). *El plano oblicuo: cuentos y diálogos* [short stories]. Madrid: Tipográfica "Europa," 1920: La cena [First published as "The Supper," trans. E. Smiley, in *Adam* (London), (July–August 1917)].—De cómo Chamisso dialogó con un aparador holandés.—Diálogo de Aquiles y Helena.—En las repúblicas del Soconusco (Memorias de un súbdito alemán).—El fraile converso (Diálogo mudo).—La reina perdida.—Lucha de patronos (En los Campos Eliseos).

——————. *El cazador: ensayos y divagaciones (1910–1921)* [short stories]. Madrid: Biblioteca Nueva, 1921: Diálogo de mi ingenio y mi conciencia (Pesadilla).

——————. *Arbol de pólvora* [short stories]. México: Imprenta Nuevo Mundo, 1953: Los Quitutos.—La Retro.

——————. "La asamblea de los animales" [short story]. "México en la cul-tura," No. 204, Suppl. *Novedades,* febrero 15, 1953, p. 3.

——————. *Quince presencias (1915–1954)* [short stories]. Colección Lite-raria Obregón, Núm. 2. México: Obregón, 1955: Las babuchas.—El rey del cocktail.—La mano del Comandante Aranda.

——————. *Las burlas veras. Segundo Ciento* [essays and short stories]. México: Tezontle, 1959: Encuentro con un diablo.

Reyes Nevares, Salvador (1922). *Frontera indecisa* [short stories]. Los Presentes, Núm. 23. México, 1955: El estilete prodigioso [First published in

"Revista mexicana de cultura," No. 374, Suppl. *El nacional,* mayo 30, 1954, pp. 3–4, 13].—La pirueta [First published in "Revista mexicana de cultura," No. 397, Suppl. *El nacional,* noviembre 7, 1954, pp. 8–9].— Algunos apuntes relativos al Monte de la Verdad.

──────. "La sala de espera" [short story]. *Anuario del cuento mexicano 1960.* México: Instituto Nacional de Bellas Artes, 1961. Pp. 186–194 [Not published elsewhere].

Riva Palacio, Vicente (1832–1896). *Los ceros: galería de contemporáneos* [short stories]. México: Imprenta de F. Díaz de León, 1882: El buen ejemplo.

──────. *Los cuentos del General* [short stories]. Madrid: Estampa y Tipografía Sucesores de Rivadeneyra, 1896 [Reprinted: "El buen ejemplo"]: La horma de su zapato [First published in *La ilustración española y americana* (Madrid), 37, No. 7 (febrero 22, 1893), 118–119].—Las honras de Carlos V.—La leyenda de un santo [First published in *La ilustración española y americana* (Madrid), 37, No. 16 (marzo 30, 1893), 285, 288].—El divorcio.—El matrimonio desigual.—La bendición de Abraham.

Rivas, Manuel Antonio de (fl. 1773). "Untitled" [short story]. *Archivo General de la Nación: Inquisición,* Tomo 1187, Fascículos 60–160v (1774).

Roa Bárcena, José María (1827–1908). *Novelas; originales y traducidas* [short stories]. México: Editorial de "La Unión"; Imprenta de F. Díaz de León y Santiago White, 1870: El hombre del caballo rucio.

──────. *Lanchitas* [legend]. México. 1877.

──────. *Varios cuentos* [short stories]. México: Imprenta de Ignacio Escalante, 1882 [Reprinted: "El hombre del caballo rucio" and "Lanchitas"]: El rey y el bufón.

Robles del Valle, Guadalupe. "No fue su hora" [short story]. "Revista de la semana," Suppl. *El universal,* julio 7, 1968, p. 4.

Rodríguez, Alfredo. "Blanco y negro" [short story]. *Revista Azul,* 2, No. 13 (enero 27, 1895), 206–207.

Rodríguez Rivera, Ramón (1850–1889). *La Llorona: cuento popular* [short story]. México. Tipografía "El Gran Libro," de J. M. Parrés y Cía., 1883.

Rojas González, Francisco (1904–1951). *Historia de un frac* [short story]. México: Editor Vargas Rea, 1930.

──────. *Cuentos de ayer y de hoy* [short stories]. México: Editorial Arte de América, 1946: Un nuevo procedimiento.—Mateo el Evangelista.

Romero, José Rubén (1890–1952). *Anticipación a la muerte* [novel]. México: Talleres Gráficos de la Nación, 1939.

Romero de Terreros [y Vinent], Manuel (Marqués de San Francisco) (1880–1968). *Florilegio* [short stories]. México: M. León Sánchez, 1909: Apólogo oriental.—La tumba desconocida.—El jardinero.

──────. *La puerta de bronce y otros cuentos* [short stories]. Guadalajara, Jalisco: Librería y Casa Editorial de Fortino Jaime, 1922: La puerta de bronce.—Similia Similibus.—Un hombre práctico.—Una partida de ajedrez.—El cofre.—Fray Baltasar.—El amo viejo.—El jade rojo.—El camino de los carboneros.—Los dos cedros.—La leyenda de Fray Gil.—El papagayo de Huichilobos [First published in *México moderno: revista de letras y arte*, 1, No. 2 (septiembre 1920), 108–113].—Luna llena.

Rosenzweig, Carmen (1925). *El reloj* [short stories]. Los Presentes, Núm. 44. México, 1956: ¡No por el de las nubes!—¡Excelencia, Excelencia!—Deudos, he muerto [First published in *Revista mexicana de literatura*, 1, No. 1 (septiembre–octubre 1955), 10–12].—El juego maravilloso.—Dos pizarrones (El reloj no tiene función).

Rubín, Luis G. (1837–1922). *Leyendas históricas mexicanas* [legends]. México, 1915: La leyenda de don Juan Manuel.

Ruiz, Cristina. "La puerta secreta" [short story]. "Revista de la semana," Suppl. *El universal*, mayo 26, 1968, p. 4.

Ruiz, Eduardo (1839–1902). *Michoacán: paisajes, tradiciones y leyendas* [legends]. II. México: Oficina de la Secretaría de Fomento, 1900: Fray Juan de San Miguel.

Rulfo, Juan (1918). *El llano en llamas* [short stories]. Letras Mexicanas, Núm. 11. México: Fondo de Cultura Económica, 1953: Luvina.

————. *Pedro Páramo* [novel]. Letras Mexicanas, Núm. 19. México: Fondo de Cultura Económica, 1955 [A draft of Chap. I published as "Un cuento," in *Las letras patrias*, No. 1 (enero–marzo 1954), 104–108. The novel was to have been called "Una estrella junto a la luna,"; then it became "Los murmullos," and finally "Pedro Páramo"].

Sainz, Gustavo (1940). "El árbol de los sátiros" [short story]. *Cuadernos del viento*, 1, No. 6 (enero 1961), 89.

————. "Toda la magia del mundo" [short story]. *Anuario del cuento mexicano 1961*. México: Instituto Nacional de Bellas Artes, 1962. Pp. 204–207 [First published in *Cuadernos de bellas artes*, 2, No. 6 (junio 1961), 10–13].

Salado Alvarez, Victoriano (1867–1931). "Historia del hombre que se hizo sabio" [short story]. *Cuentos mexicanos del siglo XIX*, ed. José Mancisidor. Colección Atenea. México: Editorial Nueva España, [1940]. Pp. 650–653.

————. *Cuentos y narraciones* [short stories]. Prologue by Ana Salado Alvarez. México: Editorial Porrúa, 1953: El fantasma.

Sánchez Cámara, Florencio (1927). *El sapófago* [short stories]. Cuadernos Literarios Lince, Núm. 6. México: Editorial Los Insurgentes, 1961: Musa fatal.—El velorio.—La variante.—El lunático.—Nominalismo.

Sánchez Galindo, Antonio. *Orden de colonización* [short stories]. México: B. Costa-Amic, Editor, 1966: Venganza en cadena.—La última revolución.—Amor mecánico.—La última sonrisa.—Orden de colonización.—El C. D.

Sánchez Zúber, Leopoldo (1925). *Marejada* [short stories]. Colección Ficción, Núm. 68. Xalapa, Veracruz: Universidad Veracruzana, 1966: La rendija.—Heliodoro.—El acróbata.

Santaella Cortés, Gustavo. "Ataque al amanecer" [short story]. "Revista de la semana," Suppl. *El universal*, julio 21, 1968, p. 4.

Sierra, Justo (1848–1912). *Cuentos románticos* [short stories]. París y México: Librería de la Vda. de Ch. Bouret, 1896 [First published among his "Conversaciones del domingo," in *El monitor republicano* (1868)]: La fiebre amarilla.—La sirena.—Incógnita.

Sigüenza y Góngora, Carlos de (1645–1700). *Paraíso occidental, plantado y cultivado por la liberal benéfica mano de los muy Cathólicos y poderosos Reyes de España Nuestros Señores, en su magnífico Real Convento de Jesús María de México* [legends]. México: Imprenta de Juan de Rivera, 1684: Lo que aconteció a una monja con un clérigo difunto.

Silva y Aceves, Mariano (1887–1937). *Arquilla de marfil* [short stories]. México: Librería de Porrúa Hermanos, 1916: Las rosas de Juan Diego.—La ruta de Aztlán.—El deseo de Juan Palomo.

Solana, Rafael (1915). *La trompeta* [short story]. México, 1941.

————. *La música por dentro* [short stories]. México: Editorial Géminis, 1943 [Reprinted: "La trompeta"]: El concierto [First published in *El hijo pródigo*, 1, No. 4 (julio 1943), 230–235].

————. *Los santos inocentes* [short stories]. México: Editorial Géminis, 1944: La piedra [First published in *El hijo pródigo*, 4, No. 15 (junio 1944), 155–158].—El arma secreta.

————. *Trata de muertos* [short stories]. México: Imprenta "Luz," 1947: Cirugía de guerra [First published in *Revista mexicana de cultura*, n.s., No. 1, Suppl. *El nacional*, abril 6, 1947, pp. 8–9].

————. *El oficleido y otros cuentos* [short stories]. México: Libro-Mex., Editores, 1960: Sansón y Dalila [First published in *América*, No. 65 (abril 1951), 12–22].—La epilitia [First published in *Siempre!*, 1, No. 3, julio 11, 1953, pp. 41, 72–74].—Diario de viaje de dos exploradores negros en busca de la tumba de los automóviles [First published in *Veracruz*, No. 55 (octubre 1954)].

Sosa, Francisco (1848–1925). *Doce leyendas de Francisco Sosa* [legends]. México: Imprenta y Litografía de Ireneo Paz, 1877: El sueño de la magnetizada.

Souto Alabarce, Arturo (1930). *La plaga del crisantemo* [short stories]. México: Imprenta Universitaria, 1960: No escondas tu cara.—La plaga del crisantemo.

Souza, Antonio (1928). *El niño y el árbol* [novelette]. Los Presentes, Núm. 17. México, 1955.

————. "La gorgona" [short story] *Cuentistas mexicanos modernos* [anthology]. ed. Emmanuel Carballo. Biblioteca Mínima Mexicana, Núm. 27. México: Libro-Mex., Editores, 1956. II, 217–221.

Tablada, José Juan (1871–1945). "Exempli gratia o fábula de los siete trovadores y de la *Revista moderna*" [fable]. *Revista moderna*, 1, No. 1 (julio 1, 1898), 2–3.

————. "De ultratumba" [short story]. *Cuentos mexicanos* [anthology]. México: Tipografía de "El Nacional," 1898. Pp. 10–14.

Taracena, Alfonso (1899). *Cuentos frente al mar* [short stories]. México: Editorial Bolívar, 1928: La expiación de la serpiente.

————. *Diez personajes extravagantes* [short stories]. México: Editorial Bolívar, 1930: El caballero de la triste figura.

—————. "La cruz de Cunduacán" [legend]. *Imaginación de México* [anthology], ed. Rafael Heliodoro Valle. Colección Austral, Núm. 477. Buenos Aires y México: Espasa-Calpe, 1945. P. 174.

Tario, Francisco [pseud. of Francisco Peláez] (1911). *La noche* [short stories]. México: Antigua Librería Robredo, 1943: La noche del féretro.—La noche del buque náufrago.—La noche del loco.—La noche del vals y el nocturno. —La noche de los cincuenta libros.—La noche de la gallina.—La noche del perro.—La noche de Margaret Rose.—La noche del muñeco.—La noche de los genios raros.—La noche del traje gris.—La noche de "La Valse".—La noche del hombre.—Mi noche.

—————. *Equinoccio* [brief sketches, aphorisms]. México, 1946.

—————. *Tapioca Inn: mansión para fantasmas* [short stories]. México: Tezontle, 1952: La polka de los Curitas.—Aureola o alvéolo [First published as "Fascinación: aureola o alvéolo," in *América*, 2, No. 63 (junio 1950), 187–206].—Usted tiene la palabra.—Ciclopropano.—Música de cabaret [brief sketches].—T. S. H.—El mar, la luna y los banqueros.—La semana escarlata.

—————. *Una violeta de más: cuentos fantásticos* [short stories]. Colección Nueva Narrativa Hispánica. México: Joaquín Mortiz, 1968: El mico.—La Vuelta a Francia.—Ave María Purísima.—Asesinato en do sostenido mayor.—El balcón [First published in *Revista de la Universidad de México*, 11, No. 12 (agosto 1957), 6–7].—Un inefable rumor.—El éxodo.— Ragú de ternera.—Fuera de programa.—Ortodoncia.—La banca vacía [First published in *Revista mexicana de literatura*, 2a Ser., 1, No. 8 (noviembre–diciembre 1956), 11–17].—Entre tus dedos helados.

Tenorio Bahena, Jorge I. "Federico Trueba" [short story]. "Revista de la semana," Suppl. *El universal*, agosto 4, 1968, pp. 4–5.

Toral Moreno, Alfonso (1914). "Angustia" [short story]. *Summa* (Guadalajara), (agosto 1954), 253–256.

—————. "Justicia onírica" [short story]. *Et caetera* (Guadalajara), 5, Nos. 17–18 (octubre 1955), 57–66.

—————. "Uxor" [short story]. *Cuentistas mexicanos modernos* [anthology], ed. Emmanuel Carballo. Biblioteca Mínima Mexicana, Núm. 26. México: Libro-Mex., Editores, 1956. I, 29–35.

Toro, Carlos (1875–1914). *El miedo: algunos cuentos* [short stories]. México: Talleres Gráficos de la S[ecretaría de] E[ducación] P[ública], 1947: El gato. —El árbol de los caracoles.—Botella de sidra.—El beso de Juana (Cuento frívolo).—El hombre artificial.—El dieciocho de mayo.—La mujer azul.— El retrato.—Cuento del futuro.—Conseja popular.—Un padre telepático.

Torres Quintero, Gregorio (1865–1934). *Cuentos colimotes: descripciones, cuentos y sucedidos* [short stories]. México: Herrero Hermanos Sucesores, 1931: El guarda virreinal.—La Barranca del Muerto.—La ciudad encantada.—El cayuco del diablo.—El montero.—El sueño del pobre y del rico.

Torres Septién, Ramiro (1913). *Sombra verde* [novel]. México, 1949.

—————. *Roquedal* [novel]. México, 1954.

Torri, Julio (1889–1970). *Ensayos y poemas* [short stories]. México: Editorial Porrúa Hermanos, 1917: La conquista de la luna.—La vida del campo.—La balada de las hojas más altas.—Era un país pobre.

————. *De fusilamientos* [short stories]. México: La Casa de España en México, 1940: El héroe.—La cocinera.—Los unicornios.

————. "Prosas dispersas" [short stories]. *Tres libros*. Letras Mexicanas. Volumen Especial. México: Fondo de Cultura Económica, 1964: El vagabundo.

Trueba, Eugenio (1921). "Cuentos" [short stories]. *Difusiones*, No. 1, Guanajuato (1951): Antesala.—Confesión al prójimo.—Un hombre respetuoso de la ley.

————. *Antesala* [short stories]. Los Presentes, Núm. 40. México, 1956 [Reprinted: "Antesala," "Confesión al prójimo"]: Los burros de San Felipe [First published in *Garabato* (Guanajuato), No. 3 (febrero 1954)].

————. *La pupila del gato* [short stories]. Guanajuato: Ediciones Llave; Universidad de Guanajuato, 1957: De la abyección.—La ley es un balbuceo.—El mal de perro, Catalina y el pianista.—Sobre documentos.

————. "Una mala mirada" [novelette]. [unpublished; written August 1966].

Turrent Rozas, Lorenzo (1903–1941). *Jack: cuentos* [short stories]. Prologue by Ermilo Abreu Gómez. Colección Cuentistas Mexicanos, Núm. 3. México: Editorial "Mundo Nuevo," 1940: Cuento de febrero.

Urquizo, Francisco L[uis] (1891–1969). *Lo incognoscible* [novel]. Madrid: Editorial V. H. Sanz Calleja, [1923].

————. *Mi tío Juan: novela fantástica* [novel]. México: Editorial Claret, 1934.

————. *H. D. T. U. P.: cuentos y narraciones* [short stories]. México: Cía. Editora Mexicana, 1935: El tesoro de Cuauhtémoc.

————. *Cuentos y leyendas* [short stories]. México: Editorial Cultura, 1945 [Reprinted: "El tesoro de Cuauhtémoc"]: La sombra.

Urzáis [Rodríguez], Eduardo (1876–1955). *Eugenia: esbozo novelesco de costumbres futuras* [novel]. Mérida, Yucatán, 1919.

Useta, Jorge [pseud. of José Ugarte]. (1880). *Espectro: veinticinco cuentos de siete colores; cuentos grotescos y caprichosos; cuentos reales; cuentos del viajero; cuentos bufones* [short stories]. Barcelona: Casa Editorial Araluce, 1932: La muerte de la pena.—El joven Godofredo y sus glándulas.—Personajes de personajes o complicaciones pirandelianas.

Valadés, Edmundo (1915). *Antípoda* [short stories]. México: Ediciones El Unicornio, 1961: El cuchillo [First published in *Cuadernos del viento*, 2, No. 13 (agosto 1961), 204–205].

Valdés, Carlos (1928). "¡Salvar al mundo!" [short story]. *Cuentistas mexicanos modernos* [anthology], ed. Emmanuel Carballo. Biblioteca Mínima Mexicana, Núm. 27. México: Libro-Mex., Editores, 1956. II, 201–213 [First published as "Intriga de ajedrez" in *Ideas de México*, 2a Ser., 2, Nos. 7–8 (septiembre–diciembre 1954), 14–22].

——————— . *Ausencias* [short stories]. Los Presentes, Núm. 10. México, 1955: Soliloquio de la calle novena.—El escritor nonato.

——————— . *Dos ficciones* [short stories]. Cuadernos del Unicornio, Núm. 5. México, 1958: Visita al zoológico [First published in *Revista mexicana de literatura*, 2a Ser., 1, No. 6 (julio–agosto 1956), 593–595].

——————— . *Dos y los muertos* [short stories]. México: Imprenta Universitaria, 1960: El último unicornio [Revised version of "El unicornio," first published in *Aventura y misterio (originales en castellano)*. Vol. VIII. México: Editorial Novaro-México, 1957. Pp. 12–20].

——————— . *El nombre es lo de menos* [short stories]. Letras Mexicanas, Núm. 70. México: Fondo de Cultura Económica, 1961: El escorpión al acecho [First published in *Cuadernos del viento*, 1, No. 1 (agosto 1960), 8–10; 1, No. 2 (septiembre 1960), 28–30].—La calle aún es nuestra.

——————— . "Una tajada de vida" [short story]. *Cuadernos del viento*, 2, No. 16 (noviembre 1961), 247–252.

Valle-Arizpe, Artemio de (1888–1961). *Vidas milagrosas* [legends]. Madrid: Tipografía Artística, 1921: Nuestra Señora de Monterrosa.

——————— . *Del tiempo pasado* [legends]. Madrid: Biblioteca Nueva, 1932: Coro de sombras.—El collar de los rubíes.—La marca de fuego.—El alacrán de Fray Anselmo [First published in *La raza* (Santo Domingo), 1931].—El Señor del veneno.—Cómo se supo en Nueva España la muerte de Carlos V.

——————— . *Cuentos del México antiguo* [legends]. Colección Austral, Núm. 53. México: Espasa-Calpe, 1939: Vida ejemplar.—Las flores del pino [First published in *Abside*, 2, No. 7 (julio 1938), 27–36].—Por ir al mal fue al bien. —El que hace daño, no espere premio.—Crimen y castigo.—La perla del Señor.

——————— . *Leyendas mexicanas* [legends]. Colección Austral, Núm. 340. México: Espasa-Calpe, 1943: La paga del fraile.—El Callejón del Muerto.— La dama viajera.—La cruz de Santa Catarina.—Lo que contó la difunta.— Las palomas.

——————— . *Amor que cayó en castigo* [legend]. Colección "Lunes," Núm. 17. México: Pablo y Henrique González-Casanova; Imprenta de B. Costa-Amic, 1945.

——————— . *En México y en otros siglos* [legends]. Colección Austral, Núm. 881. Buenos Aires y México: Espasa-Calpe, 1948: La Virgen de la Bala.— Estampa de códice.—Don Juan Manuel de Solórzano.—El compañero.

——————— . *De la Nueva España* [legends]. Colección Austral, Núm. 1278. Buenos Aires y México: Espasa-Calpe, 1956 [Reprinted: "El alacrán de Fray Anselmo" and "Cómo se supo en la Nueva España la muerte de Carlos V"]: El Tapado.

Vasconcelos, José (1882–1959). *Divagaciones literarias* [short stories]. Lectura Selecta, Núm. 5. México: Tipografía Murguía, 1919: El fusilado.

——————— . *La sonata mágica* [short stories]. Madrid: Imprenta de Juan Pueyo, 1933 [Reprinted: "El fusilado"]: La sonata mágica.—La casa imantada.

Vázquez Gómez, Esperanza G. de (d.1966?). *El misterio del estanque* [short story]. México: Imprenta Monterrubio, 1950.

Vela, Arqueles (1889). "El viaje redondo" [short story]. *Revista de revistas,* 19, No. 1024 (diciembre 15, 1929), 20–21, 56–57.

——————. *Cuentos del día y de la noche* [short stories]. México: Editorial "Don Quijote," 1945: Un crimen sin nombre.—La muchacha de las multitudes.

——————. *La volanda* [novel]. México: [Private edition; distributed by Editorial Botas], 1956.

——————. *El picaflor* [novel]. México: B. Costa-Amic, Editor, 1961.

——————. *Luzbela: novelerías* [short stories]. México: B. Costa-Amic, Editor, 1966: Luzbela.—Las tres gracias.—Los sueños.

La venganza de los difuntos: novela fantástica [novel]. México: Imprenta de Vicente García Torres, 1850 [anonymous work].

Vereo Guzmán, [Juan F.] (1896). *La rebelión de Satán: novela fantástica con final probable dedicada a Nuestra Señora de la Ironía* [novel]. México: Ediciones Populares "Atalaya," [1945?].

Vigil y Robles, Guillermo (1867). *Cuentos* [short stories]. México: Tipografía de Alejandro Marcué, 1890: La promesa.—Aventuras de una casaca.—La mutilada.

Villamil Castillo, Carlos (1911). *La venganza de los perros y otros cuentos* [short stories]. México: Ediciones Botas, 1949: La venganza de los perros.—El hombre que llevaba su alma a cuestas.—La desilusión del diablo.—El expendio de virtudes.—La decepción de la pulga.—¡Frank se ha vuelto loco!—Memorias de una lata de sardinas.

Villanueva Medina, Salvador. *Hablemos de Venus* [novel]. México: Imprenta "Cosmos," 1958.

Villaurrutia, Xavier (1903–1950). "Fragmento de sueño" [short story]. *Ulises: revista de curiosidad y crítica,* 1, No. 3 (agosto 1927), 34–38 [Republished as segment of short novel *Dama de corazones,* México: Ediciones de Ulises, 1928.].

Weil, Raúl [pseud. of María Elvira Bermúdez]. "Los centauros de Denébola" [short story]. *Madame,* 14, No. 188 (noviembre 1967), 64–69.

——————. "Vuelo en la noche" [short story]. *Madame,* 15, No. 191 (febrero 1968), 66–69.

Yáñez, Agustín (1904). *Isolda* [novelette]. México: Imprenta Universitaria, 1943.

Ymix [psued.] "Los aluxes (los amos del monte)" [short story]. "Revista de la semana," Suppl. *El universal,* junio 23, 1968, p. 4.

Zárate Ruiz, Francisco. "La defunción de la muerte" [short story]. *Revista moderna,* 1, No. 5 (octubre 1, 1898), 77–79.

——————. "La cabeza del muñeco" [short story]. *Cuentos mexicanos del siglo XIX* [anthology], ed. José Mancisdor. Colección Atenea. México: Editorial Nueva España, [1940]. Pp. 731–737.

Zavala Ruiz, Roberto. "El ángel y yo" [short story]. *Punto de partida,* 2, No. 11 (julio–agosto 1968), 25–26.

Index

DATE DUE

JUL 0 8 2000

INTERLIBRARY LOAN

APR 0 7 2000

Printed in USA

HIGHSMITH #45230